PATRI

PANAF GREAT LIVES

Patrice Lumumba

Panaf

LONDON

SBN 901787 31 0

Published by
Panaf Books Limited
243 Regent Street, London, WIR 8PN
Printed in Great Britian by
Cox & Wyman Ltd., London, Fakenham and Reading

CONTENTS

PLATES

Cover photo

Patrice Lumumba on the floor of a lorry at Ndjili Airport, Leopoldville, on 2 December 1960, after being flown in from Luluabourg. He had been captured the previous night at Port Franqui, and been beaten up by Mobutu's troops.

ABBREVIATIONS

ABAKO	Association des Bakongo pour l'Unification l'Expansion et la Defense de la Kilonga. Formed 1950. Led by Joseph Kasavubu.
ANC	Armée Nationale Congolaise.
BALUBAKAT	The Baluba Association of Katanga. Founded in 1957. Led by Joseph Sendwe.
CONAKAT	Confederation of Tribal Associations of Katanga. First President, Godefroid Munungo. Handed over presidency to Moise Tshombe in 1959. Supported by Union Minière.
CNL	Comité National de Libération.
CSK	Comité Spécial du Katanga.
EEC	European Economic Community
EVOLUÉS	Congolese who 'evolved' through education to become accepted by the Belgians as the new westernized élite of Congolese society – the emergent middle class.
FÉDÉCOL	Congolese Federation of the Middle Classes.

FORMINIÈRE	Société Internationale Forestière et Minière du Congo.
LUKA	A tribal political party affiliated to PNP.
MNC	Mouvement National Congolais. Founded by Lumumba in 1958. Split in 1959 resulted in *MNC Lumumba* and *MNC Kalondji*.
ONUC	United Nations Operational Command.
PNP	Le Parti National du Progrès. A pro-Belgian party founded in 1959.
PSA	Parti Solidaire Africain. Antoine Gizenga, President, and Pierre Mulele, Secretary-General.
UNION MINIÈRE	Union Minière du Haut Katanga. A major mining enterprise in the Congo.
UNO	United Nations Organization.

CHRONOLOGY

1925   Lumumba born in Stanleyville in Orientale Province. A member of the Batelela tribe, a sub-group of the Mongo tribe.

1955   Visited Belgium on a government-sponsored tour.
Chairman or secretary of seven associations including the Association des Evolués. Active member of Cercle Liberal de Stanleyville.

1957   Employed in Stanleyville Post Office.
Became sales manager of Bracongo Brewery in Leopoldville.

1958   Attended the First All-African Peoples' Conference in Accra, Ghana. Became member of the Steering Committee.
On return to Leopoldville held public meeting to report on the Conference.
29 December. Announced new programme for the MNC based on the Accra Resolutions, and declared that independence would be not a gift from Belgium, but a fundamental right of the Congolese people.

1959   4 January. Riots in Leopoldville; over 50 killed and some 200 injured. ABAKO proscribed, and leaders arrested. No action taken against MNC.
Lumumba travelled around Belgium addressing meetings, appearing on TV, etc., preaching anti-colonialism and advocating the release of ABAKO leaders.
13 January. Belgium's de-colonization proposals announced in 'Declaration Gouvernementale'; Congolese to be led to independence 'graduellement et progressivement'.
1 November. Lumumba arrested in Stanleyville and charged with provoking a riot. Sentenced to six months' imprisonment.

9

1960   20 January. Belgian–Congolese Round Table Conference opened in Brussels. Association of Congolese students in Belgium urged Congolese delegations to present a united Front to the Belgians. Purpose of the Conference was to set up political structures in the Congo to form the provisional constitution for an independent Congo. Attended by representatives of Congolese parties and members of the Belgian parliament and government. Closed on 20 February.

Lumumba released from prison to attend the Conference.

11–25 May. Elections held in the Congo. Victory for Lumumba and the MNC, with 74 out of the 137 seats in the House of Representatives.

10 May. La Loi Fondamentale sur les Structures de Congo (Basic Law) passed by the Belgian Senate, providing for the Constitution of the new Republic of the Congo.

24 June. First National Government formed with Kasavubu as Head of State and Lumumba as Prime Minister.

29 June. Belgian–Congolese Treaty of Friendship signed.

30 June. Independent Republic of the Congo proclaimed. Mutinies among Force Publique.

11 July. Tshombe proclaimed the Independent State of Katanga.

Seizure of Matadi and Leopoldville airports by Belgian troops.

12 July. Appeal by Congolese government for UN military assistance against Belgian aggression.

15 July. First UN troops (Tunisian and Ghanaian) landed in the Congo.

Arrival of further Belgian troops in Katanga.

22 July. UN Security Council called on Belgium to withdraw its troops from the Congo.

Lumumba visited the USA and various Independent Africa States.

7–8 August. Lumumba in Accra, Ghana. Signed a

secret Agreement with President Kwame Nkrumah providing for a political Union between the Congo and Ghana. This was to be the nucleus for a Union of African States.

12 August. UN Secretary-General, Hammarskjold, arrived in Katanga with a token UN force.

25–30 August. Conference of Independent African States held in Leopoldville.

5 September. Kasavubu broadcast his dismissal of Lumumba as prime minister.

Lumumba broadcast his dismissal of Kasavubu as Head of State, and called on the people and army for support.

UN forces closed all major airports in the Congo, except for UN planes.

6 September. UN closed Leopoldville radio station and prevented Lumumba from broadcasting.

Chamber of Representatives revoked both dismissals.

8 September. Senate gave Lumumba a vote of confidence.

9 September. Lumumba announced he was Chief of State and Supreme Commander of the National Army.

Kasavubu rejected votes of both the Senate and the Chamber of Representatives.

11 September. President of the Chamber of Representatives and the Acting President of the Senate informed the UN that the votes of their separate bodies constituted a sovereign determination of a renewal of confidence in Lumumba's government, and an annulment of Kasavubu's ordinance.

Joseph Ileo announced the formation of a new government.

Reopening of the radio station by the UN.

12 September. Arrest of Lumumba on orders of Kasavubu and Ileo. Later released.

13 September. A joint meeting of the Chamber of Representatives and the Senate voted full powers to

Lumumba by 88 votes to 5 with 3 abstentions.

14 September. Kasavubu declared the joint session illegal, and adjourned parliament for one month.

Broadcast by Colonel Mobutu, Army Chief of Staff stating that he was 'neutralizing' both Kasavubu and Lumumba and that the ANC (Armée Nationale Congolaise) was assuming power until 30 December 1960.

Lumumba confined to house and guarded by UN troops.

23 September. Kwame Nkrumah's address to the Fifteenth General Assembly of the UN in New York on the Congo situation. Recommended an African solution to the Congo problem with full support of the UN.

11 October. Attempts by Mobutu to arrest Lumumba failed.

10 November. Credentials Committee of the UN recommended the seating of the Kasavubu delegation. Lumumba's delegation rejected.

22 November. Recommendation accepted by the UN General Assembly.

27 November. Lumumba asked for UN aircraft to take him to Stanleyville. Request refused.

Lumumba escaped from Leopoldville by car, and made for Stanleyville.

30 November. Arrested at Mweka near Port Francqui. Taken to Leopoldville.

7 December. Meeting of Security Council called to consider implications of his arrest.

12 December. Antoine Gizenga announced the formation of a new government of the Congo in Stanleyville.

20 December. Economic blockade instituted by the Leopoldville government against Orientale Province.

25 December. Stanleyville government troops seized Kivu Province.

1961 3-7 January. Casablanca Conference to decide whether the African States, particularly Ghana,

UAR, Guinea and Mali should withdraw their troops from the Congo.

17 January. News of the transfer of Lumumba, Okito and Mpolo to Katanga.

10 February. Katangan government announced the 'escape' of the prisoners.

13 February. News of the deaths given at press conference held by Munungo, Katangan Minister of the Interior.

1971   Republic of Zaire proclaimed.

PREFACE

LUMUMBA was not even in the prime of life when he was murdered by the agents of imperialism and neocolonialism early in 1961. He had anticipated death for some time. Yet it was not advanced age which was laying its icy hands upon him, but the claws and fangs of the enemies of the African Revolution who were thirsting for his blood. His last testament, in the form of a letter to his wife, Pauline, shows his courageous and indomitable spirit:

My dear wife,

I am writing these words not knowing whether they will reach you, when they will reach you, and whether I shall still be alive when you read them. All through my struggle for the independence of my country, I have never doubted for a single instant the final triumph of the sacred cause to which my companions and I have devoted all our lives. But what we wished for our country, its right to an honourable life, to unstained dignity, to independence without restrictions, was never desired by the Belgian imperialists and their Western allies, who found direct and indirect support, both deliberate and unintentional, amongst certain high officials of the United Nations, that organization in which we placed all our trust when we called on its assistance.

They have corrupted some of our compatriots and bribed others. They have helped to distort the truth and bring our independence into dishonour. How could I speak otherwise? Dead or alive, free or in prison by order of the imperialists it is not I myself who count. It is the Congo, it is our poor people for whom independence has been transformed into a cage from beyond whose confines the outside world looks on us, sometimes with kindly sympathy but at other times with joy and pleasure. But my faith will remain unshakeable. I know and I feel in my heart that sooner or later my people will rid themselves of all their enemies, both internal and external, and that they will rise as one man to say No to the degradation and shame of colonialism, and regain their dignity in the clear light of the sun.

We are not alone. Africa, Asia and the free liberated people from all corners of the world will always be found at the side of the millions of Congolese who will not abandon the struggle until the day when there are no longer any colonialists and their mercenaries in our country. As to my children, whom I leave and whom I may never see again, I should like them to be told that it is for them, as is it for every Congolese, to accomplish the sacred task of reconstructing our independence and our sovereignty: for without dignity there is no liberty, without justice there is no dignity, and without independence there are no free men.

Neither brutality, nor cruelty nor torture will ever bring me to ask for mercy, for I prefer to die with my head unbowed, my faith unshakeable and with profound trust in the destiny of my country, rather than live under subjection and disregarding sacred principles. History will one day have its say, but it will not be the history that is taught in Brussels, Paris, Washington or in the United Nations, but the history which will be taught in the countries freed from imperialism and its puppets. Africa will write her own history, and to the north and south of the Sahara, it will be a glorious and dignified history.

Do not weep for me, my dear wife. I know that my country, which is suffering so much, will know how to defend its independence and its liberty. Long live the Congo! Long live Africa!

PATRICE

16

INTRODUCTION

THE revolt of the submerged masses of the oppressed and exploited African workers and peasants against colonial domination threw up many leaders. These men and women who took over the leadership of the national movements were brave, resourceful and energetic. They revealed great talent as organizers. As orators they were second to none, for speech became an important weapon in keeping the cohesion necessary for a national Front of all classes against the colonizing power. Despite the leaders having different backgrounds and different temperaments they had one thing in common. They were men of action. The sum total of their ideas crystallized around the simple and easily understood slogan of political independence.

There is however some truth in the statement that a feature of the national movement in this phase of the pre-independence struggle was its low ideological content. Few of the leaders really understood the historic process involved, the criss-crossing of various currents, the intricate relationship between economics and politics, the ramifications of international finance capital and the new historical forms which had emerged. Even fewer grasped the fact that a new era of life and death struggle had opened up between the new and the old, between socialism and capitalism, and that the decadent forces in their death agony were in the process of being swept away. On the crucial question of what society would emerge after independence, whether it would be based on capitalism or socialism few gave a forthright answer. To preserve unity of the national Front, the leaders had to postpone such questions until after independence. Some of them honestly gave it no thought, for they were up to the neck organizing for independence.

This explains partly what happened to the entire

leadership which the people threw up in the phase of the national struggle for freedom. With independence they became presidents, prime ministers, M P's, district governors, heads of civil service departments or directors of state trading corporations. They took over to become an integral part of the state machinery designed by the colonial masters to operate the capitalist system. In the process of Africanizing it, they enlarged and perfected it. It thus now became their job to squeeze for their former colonial masters super profits from the sinews, muscles, sweat and tears of the toiling masses. A great deal of pomp, ceremony and ostentation surrounds many a Premier and President in Africa, Asia and Latin America. Yet this cannot hide the naked fact that these men thrown up by the oppressed and exploited masses to free and liberate them have themselves become oppressors and exploiters. Hastings Banda, Joseph Mobutu and Houphouet-Boigny, for example, have amassed fortunes. From leaders of national liberation movements, they have become glorified managers and foremen for their former colonial masters. In order to squeeze out the maximum it has become their job to exhort the already over-burdened and suffering masses to work harder, using the whip, the rope and the gun when other methods fail to get the desired results.

From honourable and dignified positions as leaders of the people, they could have risen to lofty heights, for the sky is the limit for those who draw their inspiration and strength from the inexhaustible reservoir of peoples' struggles and battles. Consciously, or otherwise, they have changed course and today some of these leaders have degenerated into wretched, pitiable and pathetic servants of their former colonial masters.

But there were leaders, though rare, within the camp of the African national liberation movement who understood. Patrice Lumumba, head of the Movement National Congolais (M N C) Congo's First Prime Minister, was one of them. It is indeed remarkable that the Congolese people should have thrown up such a man, for the whole state machinery of the Belgian Government, their whole mission system of education, was designed to stunt and frustrate any independent and creative development of the Congolese people. No colonial power was so effectively able to cut off an entire generation of people from the main stream of world civilization. Thus the whole orientation of the development of the evolués, was to prevent this rising section of the Congolese intelligentsia from coming into contact with any national or scientific political ideas. The vast majority of the few Congolese who were admitted to schools did not go beyond primary level, and they were educated with the one purpose, that they would play their role in the mental enslavement of the Congolese people.

Lumumba in the early phase was, like any other Congolese leader, infected with the disease of slave mentality, and looked to the Belgians for leadership and guidance. But at a certain stage of development, coinciding with the increased growth of political consciousness of his people, he broke through. He cut the umbilical cord that bound him ideologically with his masters and oppressors, and as he became more and more enmeshed with the people, his confidence in their strength grew, as did his conviction that they and they alone would constitute the force that could liberate the Congo. He arrived at the conclusion from hard and bitter experience that only armed struggle of the people would dislodge the Belgians in Katanga. He had already reached this conclusion even before his election as Prime Minister. This brought him into direct collision with imperialists and their puppets. They marked him down, and worked tirelessly and indefatigably to bring about his destruction. Only after they had engineered a murder so foul, so brutal, as to revolt the conscience of mankind did they allow themselves any rest.

Born of Christian parents, Lumumba like any intelligent and promising youth largely educated himself. He read widely and voraciously, assimilating some of the most advanced ideas that modern society could make available. He was aware of the writings of the classical authors. His interest ranged from philosophy to economics and law. His alert mind was always receptive to new ideas. His horizons went beyond the confines of the Congo and that is why he so readily embraced Pan Africanism. The arsenal of human knowledge which he was able to absorb he later put at the disposal of the people through the MNC, which he founded and whose leader he became.

In the middle of the nineteen-fifties most leaders of nationalist movements or opinion both in the English and French speaking colonies talked vaguely about freedom and the people. But Lumumba was one of the few people who was aware of classes and class struggle. Even before the historic Accra Conference of 1958 which brought about a qualitative change in his political thinking, he showed remarkable insight when in his book, *Congo My People*, published posthumously, he asserted that the root of national oppression was not political but economic. At a time when a section of the national movement leadership was regarding the white people as synonymous with exploiters, he pointed out that what the Congolese workers were subjected to was no different from what the workers in Belgium and the rest of Europe were experiencing. Implicit in this then, was that workers suffer from exploitation whether they be white, black or brown. Looking at problems from such a standpoint, Lumumba could not possibly be a racialist. Many a nationalist leader took over the racism of the colonial master and became anti-white. Not so Lumumba. Before 1960 he called for cooperation between the Belgian and the Congolese people. After independence when the machinations of the Belgian administrators, Belgian companies and white settlers in the Congo aimed at disruption and his downfall, Lumumba still made a distinction between the Belgian Government, the former rulers, and the Belgian people. He wanted the former to go because their presence and activities were incompatible with national sovereignty. At the same time he appealed to the Belgian teachers to remain, because they were needed.

Revolutionary movements bring out both the best and the worst in those who are involved. Among revolutionaries are produced men and women of action who are also thinkers, writers and poets, organizers and soldiers. The national liberation movements too were in the process of producing this type of person before the blight of corruption, either through power or money, stunted their growth.

Lumumba attracted the attention of his Belgian and Congolese colleagues as an activist who had a fantastic store of energy. He was on the go all the time either organizing, writing, or making speeches. During his stay in Stanleyville before 1958, he was either the secretary or chairman of seven organizations. He was a prolific writer and his restless spirit found a creative outlet in poetry. If Lumumba thought rapidly, he also felt deeply and intensely. For him, the elimination of oppression was not just an intellectual exercise, but something about which he felt passionately. He was equally moved by the plight and degradation of women in Congolese society and was angered that his fellow evolués treated their wives as servants or serfs. The terrible and, inhuman conditions in prisons disgusted him, and he did all he could to expose them and the police brutalities perpetrated against the people.

Lumumba had enemies. Many of those who professed to be his friends while he was alive have since his murder tried to vilify him. They now say that he was a dictator once in power, that he was impulsive, obstinate, and refused to listen to their gratuitous advice. These are dishonest attempts to sidetrack the basic issue. For the chief reason that Lumumba made enemies was the stand he took on the fundamental issue of whether the independence of the Congo was to be real or a sham, and whether the political freedom of the Congo would also lead to economic independence or the entrenchment of the capitalist exploitation of foreign monopolies. When Lumumba made his choice, his action acted as a catalyst. It brought all the elements and forces outwardly diverse and unconnected to rise to the surface. This stand forced them to show their hands openly, and history has seldom seen such a network of conspiracy whose threads connected Washington, Brussels, Paris, London, Salisbury, Lisbon and Pretoria. The antennae of international finance capital reached out to feel and later connect their agents in the Congo in Moise Tshombe, Joseph Kasavubu, Joseph

Ileo and Mobutu and the lesser pawns like Justin Bomboko and Albert Kalondji. They all united with the avowed object of bringing about the downfall of the Congo's first legally elected Government. In the eyes of international monopoly capital, Lumumba by his behaviour and utterances in putting the interests of the people first and foremost had committed the most unpardonable crime in their eyes, and endangered their economic interests.

In the end this unholy alliance destroyed Lumumba, – but only just, and not without a fight that has few parallels in modern history. It takes a crisis whether it be on a battlefield, in an organization or in the field of politics to reveal just what mettle a man or a woman is made of. During the last hundred days of Lumumba's life his enemies produced crisis after crisis which descended wave upon wave on his youthful shoulders. But he rose to them and fought the enemies who created them. He challenged the traitors who closed on him like a pack of howling human dogs as well as his trusted friends who turned overnight into jack-asses.

Within a few weeks of his premiership, the forces of reaction engineered a revolt among the soldiers of the Force Publique; there followed the secession of the provinces of Katanga and Kasai; the United Nations became an occupying power; and the coups of Kasavubu and Mobutu took place. Lumumba, the Prime Minister of the Congo, was arrested and was refused the use of his own airport and radio by foreign troops.

He broke through the siege and encirclement on more than one occasion and turned the tables on his enemies. His final dash was to Stanleyville where the people had decided that the only way to liberate the Congo was by armed struggle, for all other methods of struggle had failed. Had he reached his destination, who knows, the history of the Congo perhaps would have taken a different course. But he was captured, and then hell broke loose for the Judases spared no efforts to break his spirit. They insulted, tormented, jeered and abused him and his companions. They starved and tortured him. He knew that these traitors had become beasts and would only be satisfied with his blood. Yet in all this long trial to test his beliefs and his devotion to his cause, he retained his calmness and dignity. Others of lesser calibre would have cracked up under the pressure of such physical and nerve shattering pain. Lumumba stood up against his persecutors and torturers because he understood that it was the cause that was being tested and put on trial. Persecution and torture convinced him even more of the rightness of his cause, and when he finally fell, his hand was still clutching the flag. He died, with head unbowed, the belief in the cause unshaken.

To destroy the cause, it is necessary to assassinate the character of the person who symbolized the cause. Lumumba's open enemies and his false friends never miss a chance to point out that he was once imprisoned for embezzling post office funds. Yet a chief trait in his character was his rigid honesty, both in his personal and political life. In fact he belongs to that group of African leaders like Kwame Nkrumah, Sékou Touré and Julius Nyerere who refuse to be corrupted. The bourgeoisie believe that every man has a price and at a particular ceiling he is prepared to sell himself. It is no secret that many African Presidents, Prime Ministers, and top layers of the bureaucracy have large deposits in foreign banks when their own people are starving, without means of livelihood, without hope of a future. These leaders have been corrupted. Imperialism believed that Lumumba would be like others and that he too would put his country and the honour of his people up for sale. But they were mistaken. He would have no truck with any scheme which would have brought him personal wealth, and dishonour to his people. The imperialists summed up Lumumba before he could sum up them. They realized that as head of the Congolese people, he could be a real threat, for his idealism, his frightening dedication which they branded as fanaticism could radiate throughout Africa, to inspire the downtrodden masses and at the same time expose the leaders who had been corrupted.

Well known is Lumumba's letter to Pauline his wife, his life-long companion, written while the shadow of death hovered round him. Written under the greatest of stress, it showed Lumumba still undaunted and full of optimism for the future. But less known is his poem published just after his death, entitled 'Morning in the heart of Africa'. It shows his sensitivity, at the harshness, cruelty and suffering inflicted on Africa as well as his unconquerable optimism that the new world to end this was being born with the approaching dawn.

The following translated extracts convey the theme:

> For a thousand years, you, negro, suffered like a beast,
> Your ashes strewn to the wind that roams the desert,
> Your tyrants built lustrous magic temples,
> To preserve your soul, preserve your suffering
>
> Barbaric right of fist, and a white right to a whip,
> You had the right to die, you could also weep,
> Hard torches of the sun will shine for us again,
> They'll dry the tears in your eyes and spittle on your face,
> The moment when you will break the chains, the heavy fetters,
> The evil cruel times will go, never to come again,
> A free gallant Congo will arise from the black soil,
> A free and gallant Congo. . . .
>
> The dawn is here my brother, dawn look in the air,
> A new morning breaks out in old Africa. . . .

24

I

GENESIS OF THE CONGOLESE
NATIONAL MOVEMENT

LUMUMBA was born in 1925 and grew up among the evolués of Stanleyville, in the era of the twilight of imperialism. The Western European powers who in 1884 at the Berlin Conference had cynically agreed amongst themselves to carve up the entire continent of Africa had emerged from the second imperialist war of 1939–45 weak and exhausted. As early as the beginning of this century, far sighted thinkers characterized this period as an epoch of colonial uprising and proletarian revolution. The leaders to head these movements were just being born, but socialist thinkers were able to make their prediction because of their understanding of the inexorable working of certain historical laws. The storms of colonial uprisings brewing for decades finally broke with intensity and fury on this continent of Africa in the fifties. It was these storms that threw up in the process leaders of heroic stature and proportions.

The people push to the forefront leaders at a time when they themselves are taking rapid strides forward. This could be during periods of awakening, of class struggle, or when class struggle reaches its zenith in the period of revolution. It is precisely those individuals who in this period are able to sense and then express the moods and apirations of the people and who are able to channel the collective energies to an agreed common goal who are propelled forward. It is this that they become leaders of the people.

But independent of the leaders themselves, reacting on them as well as on the people, are certain forces to which the genesis of the national movement including that of the Congo can be traced. What the Congo went through in the fifties and sixties was but a part of a world wide movement embracing the three continents of Asia, Africa and Latin

25

America. The peoples in these continents had different languages, culture traditions and religions. Yet what happened in Bolivia or India, revealed a similar pattern to what was taking place in the Congo. What united them all was that they were subjected to the same forces of capitalism, in its decaying phase of imperialism. In essence it was basically a revolt against the capitalist system although the form it took was a national movement fighting against the colonial oppressors.

Lumumba grew up in an age where the capitalist mode of production was still the dominant one in Africa and also the world. However, by the time he began to mature, the capitalist system was challenged and confronted by a superior form of social organization – the socialist system. In this phase of its decay and decline, the capitalist system can offer mankind very little. It has now become a fetter and a millstone round mankind's neck, slowing the forward march of humanity. Yet the greatest critics of the bourgeoisie, the two who worked relentlessly to bring about its downfall, Marx and Engels, paid tribute to its historical role and its achievement. They delineated the interplay of economic processes at work for as they said, 'The bourgeoisie has through its exploitation of the world market given a cosmopolitan character to production and consumption in every country. To the great chagrin of the Reactionists, it has drawn from under the feet of industry the national ground on which it stood. All old established national industries have been destroyed or are daily being destroyed. They are dislodged by new industries, whose introduction becomes a life and death question for all civilized nations, by industries that no longer work up indigenous raw material drawn from the remotest zones; industries whose products are consumed, not only at home, but in every quarter of the globe. In place of the old wants, satisfied by the production of the country, we find new wants, requiring for their satisfaction the products of distant lands and climes. In place of the old local and national seclusion and self-sufficiency, we have intercourse in every direction, universal inter-dependence of nations.'[1] Just what impact capitalism had on the feudal and tribal economies of Africa, Asia and Latin America can be seen by the following statement: 'The bourgeoisie, by the rapid improvement of all instruments of production, by the facilitated means of communication, draws all, even the most barbarian, nations into civilization. The cheap prices of its commodities are the heavy artillery with which it batters down all Chinese walls, with which it forces the barbarians' intensely obstinate hatred of foreigners, to capitulate. It compels all nations, on pain of extinction, to adopt the bourgeois mode of production. . . . Just as it has made the country dependent on the towns, so it has made barbarian and semi-barbarian countries dependent on the civilized ones, nations of peasants on nations of bourgeois. . . . Independent, or but loosely connected, provinces with separate interests, laws, governments and systems of taxation, became lumped together into one nation, with one government, one code of law, one national class-interest, one frontier and customs-tariff.'[2]

The Communist Manifesto, joint work of Marx and Engels, then proceeded to show just where the bourgeoisie contributed to the development of mankind. 'The bourgeoisie, during its rule of scarce one hundred years, has created more massive and more colossal productive forces than have all preceding generations together. Subjection of Nature's forces to man, machinery, application of chemistry to industry and agriculture, steam-navigation, railways, electric telegraphs, clearing of whole continents for cultivation, canalization of rivers, whole populations conjured out of the ground – what earlier century had even a presentiment that such productive forces slumbered in the lap of social labour?'[3]

Whether the individual entrepreneur desired these changes is not an issue. The bourgeois was the initiator of a process, but in a sense he was also its prisoner. He brought into the world the modern working class and this was to prove his undoing. But the capitalist could not help himself. He could not stop the growth of the proletariat just as he could not stop the rising of the sun. He needed the working class just as he needed air and water to survive. He thus brought about the sharpest antagonism hitherto known between classes, for this was a contradiction between socialist production, a distinct feature of capitalism and individual appropriation. This contradiction as predicted by the fathers of modern scientific socialism was resolved when the working class overthrew the bourgeoisie in Russia in 1917. Other countries have followed, notably China, Vietnam and Cuba and today over two-fifths of the world have become part of the socialist world system.

The Manifesto was written in 1848 but scarcely fifty years later, profound changes took place in the inner organism of capitalism. The changes were of a qualitative nature, and the process became known as imperialism. Lenin in his celebrated book, *Imperialism: the highest phase of capitalism* analysed this new phenomenon and revealed four of its distinct characteristics. He stated that if it were necessary to give the briefest possible definition of imperialism, we should say: 'Imperialism is the monopoly stage of capitalism.'

Its five basic features are:

1. The concentration of production and capital and its development to such a high stage that it has created monopolies which play a decisive role in economic life.
2. The merging of bank capital with industrial capital.
3. The export of capital as distinct from the export of commodities.
4. The formation of international monopolist combines which share the world amongst themselves.
5. The territorial division of the world.

The 'Scramble for Africa' which took place towards the end of the nineteenth century, involved the final division of Africa. In future if there was to be any further occupation by a colonizing power, it could be only redivision. This partition of Africa was agreed upon by leading Western powers at the Berlin Conference in 1884–85, and it was then that King Leopold of Belgium was given the Congo as his personal private property. All the land he could clear was to belong to him. The carving up of Africa meant that the

28

continent was not only to become part of the economic system of capitalism, but was also to come under the political authority of Western Europe. Political oppression together with the capitalist system of exploitation laid the foundation for the rise of the modern national movement, including that of the Congo.

A distinguishing feature of this phase of colonization was the political domination of a few industrialized States over peoples in countries who were essentially peasants living under conditions of feudalism or tribalism. But its a feature of capitalist development that it uproots the peasantry. The development of capitalism in Western Europe took five centuries and during this time, the peasants were systematically expropriated from the land. It was these landless peasants who provided the labour for the bourgeoisie to run the factories. It was they, who having been permanently urbanized, formed the modern working class, the proletariat, destined to play a revolutionary role in the transformation of society.

The feudal and tribal economies of the colonized people of Africa were attacked from two sides. First, by trade with the accompanying money economy. Secondly, by colonialism and the introduction of compulsory taxation, and compulsory, often unpaid, labour. What imperialist conquest did was to destroy that equilibrium which existed in tribal and feudal societies from time immemorial. These societies in the past experienced wars, rebellions, famines. They conquered or were conquered. But these did not affect the basic economic structure of the relationship of classes. These remained the same, despite changes in the political leadership or government. This equilibrium on the negative side brought about stagnation, and this retarded the further development of the productive forces in society. What colonial domination did was not only to rob the people of their freedom, but to destroy this equilibrium. Nowhere was this more evident than in the dispossession of the peasant from the land.

The colonies became an integral part of the entire system of capitalism. But the character of colonial domination was such that it prevented the growth of industry in the colonies.

Since the base of the modern bourgeoisie is industry, the choking of its growth meant the stunting of the growth of the national bourgeoisie. If however industries were established in the colonies, these were owned by the colonialists; that is, the monopolist bourgeoisie. What this meant in fact was that the growth of the working class in the colonies was faster than the growth of the national bourgeoisie. It has been said that the national bourgeoisie is weak in Africa, in that its involvement in the productive processes in society is virtually nil. The bourgeoisie is not the captain of the national industry. On the other hand the interplay of economic forces of capitalism rendered the peasants landless. Large tracts of land were seized and handed over to monopolist companies, the white settlers, or to the mission stations. From this arose the plantation economy geared to satisfy the needs of the European market. This led to the wholesale expropriation of the peasantry. The methods of driving the peasants from their land, uprooting them for good in Africa was not fundamentally different from what took place in Europe. There was the same harshness, brutality, fraud and corruption where the State machinery in favour of the rich came down on the small peasant to ruin and finally expropriate him. But the essential difference was that while the landless peasant went to join the ranks of the working class in the cities, his African counterpart had no industries in the cities to absorb him and to make use of his labour. The jobs in the industries, mines and plantations were few, and formed an insignificant percentage of the working force. The peasant thus driven from the land, went to the cities only to be driven back, because as there was no employment, he faced starvation.

Cities however did arise, but these were essentially centres of administration, that is supporting a population engaged in the services sector. These admnistrators thus consumed the surplus produced by the workers and peasants. The only exception were those cities that grew around the mines. Here there was a percentage of the population in the cities engaged in production. But the mines, large plantations and factories that did spring up were owned by monopolist combines. The surpluses generated were seized by the capitalist and syphoned abroad to benefit the few in London, Paris, Lisbon, New York and Brussels. The colonial administration saw to it that this process was not disturbed in any way.

Further, imperialism where it established no industry itself saw to it that none grew from the oppressed people themselves. For if the indigenous bourgeoisie is to engage directly in production and to own its means, it is necessary for it to have (a) labour (b) capital. There was enough of the former, but little of the latter. For capital implies a surplus, and this can only come from primitive accumulation. But this state of affairs implies ownership of private property, and particularly in Africa, the ownership of land; and it is this which the colonial masters refused to grant. When accumulation took the form of private ownership of cattle and sheep then campaigns were conducted under the guise of scientific farming to limit the stock.

The contradiction then is that while the capitalist economy of the colonial powers undermined the tribal and feudal societies, the colonial powers used the entire machinery as well as the financial power of the monopolies to stunt the growth of capitalist relations. Yet it is precisely this growth of production that makes it possible for the modern state to arise.

The principal trade, the production and supply of raw materials, was in the hands of foreigners. Even the retail foreign trade was in the hands of outsiders, who were either Syrians, Lebanese, Asians, or Europeans. If modern methods of production were introduced it was only in the sector where there was much profit to be had as for instance in mining. The rest of the sections of the economy remained underdeveloped, and no attempt was made to establish a self-reliant internal economy. If there was centralization it was to the extent that the rulers were able to collect taxes or extract forced labour. A capitalist economy for its optimum operation requires the development of communications as well as electric power. This was introduced, but developed only sufficiently to facilitate the exploitation of minerals and other raw materials. If roads, railways, ports and power

31

stations were constructed it was only so that the raw materials so extracted could easily be transported, and manufactured goods be brought in. The rest of the country just languished in utter backwardness.

The capitalist system creates its own superstructure to facilitate its operations. Out of it have arisen political institutions like parliament, municipal councils, based on adult franchise. From this has also grown the modern educational and judicial system, the latter with its civil and criminal law. This was to be uniform in the whole country. The capitalist state is essentially secular in orientation. Under this system the workers as a result of struggle acquired rights such as that to form trade unions or the right to strike. The relationship between an employee and employer is a civil one. As a result of frequent human intercourse, a common language also arises. It is out of the interaction of these and other forces that a nation state arises. Historically the nation state has been the creation of the bourgeoisie.

But imperialism in the colonies clamped down. The oppressed in the colonies had no franchise, had no freedom of speech and were denied the right to form trade unions. The laws too were feudal in nature in that a worker was treated as a criminal if he failed to turn up for work. There were only a handful of schools and these were in the hands of the churches. The political organizations until almost the end were proscribed. The chiefs who had now been transformed into instruments of oppression were given power to implement customary law; chiefs of different tribes implemented different laws and this prevented the growth of a uniform legal system. Likewise the growth of a national language was suppressed or discouraged and the people of different parts of the colonized country could only converse through the language of the colonizer.

The peasant who formed the bulk of the population thus suffered national oppression. Yet he was taxed although he had no representation. He was sucked into a system that ground him down further and further into poverty and which closed every opportunity for advancement. He saw little future for his sons, for the land could not support them all. If they were lucky to find jobs in the mines or farms, they usually returned not with wealth but with incurable sickness which sent them to their graves before their time. He himself was incessantly harassed and hounded by the tax collector or by other petty officials or bureaucrats who demanded money all the time.

A society that brought him increasing misery and poverty, a society that offered him neither security nor hope nor future meant that such a society had to be changed. More so as he could see that this society which was capable of offering the very things that he and his people were being denied and for which they were aspiring, was being fleeced by the colonizer. A change was necessary if they were to survive. Land hunger, unemployment, national oppression, the result of the operation of the capitalist system and imperialist domination, matters which had become questions of life and death, had pushed the people forward. They groped for methods and organizations to show them a way out. It was a time of bitter trial and error resulting in untold suffering. At a certain stage in the development of their own consciousness they created the national movement. Originally it came from the intellectuals, that is from their sons and daughters for whom they had managed to squeeze some degree of education. The same fervour and passion, the same trust and hope which they had reposed in earlier organization they now gave to the national movement.

2

CONGOLESE PEASANTRY

THE geographical situation, its mineral resources, its climatic conditions were three principal factors responsible for the Congo being integrated into the modern capitalist system to a degree not easily found elsewhere in Africa. Its proximity to Europe, its navigable rivers, made it easier and cheaper to transport the much needed raw materials to

Belgium. Its rich mineral resources include copper, diamonds, tin and uranium. Its climate is such as to make possible a variety of tropical products. The main crops grown are rubber, palm oil and coffee. Land was also set aside for cattle ranching. However, it was the production of cotton that brought the entire Congolese peasantry face to face with the capitalist economy, wreaking havoc with traditional farming. The cotton interests were so strong that legislation was passed to make it compulsory for the peasant to perform labour for sixty days a year to cultivate this crop. At one stage there were 700,000 small cotton growers. By 1957 this number occupied 331,774 hectares (1 hect: equals 2.471 acres) producing 129,829 tons. The exploitation of the small peasant farmer caused rural discontent and this gave impetus to the national movement.

Although the Berlin Conference of 1884–85 awarded the whole of the Congo to King Leopold of Belgium as his personal property, he alone could not exploit the vast natural resources of this rich country. He thus invited representatives of monopoly capital to move in. And they did so in a big way. In 1906, three international companies were set up which were to dominate the economy of the Congo. They were the Compagnie du Chemin de Fer du Bas-Congo (BCK); the Société Internationale Forestière et Minière du Congo (Forminière); the Union Minière du Haut-Katanga.

Of significance however at the turn of the century was the entry of American finance capital. Leopold invited forestry and mining companies into the Congo and granted them extensive mineral rights. Another Corporation, the American Congo Company was granted rights to work rubber. The former had only rights in the diamond producing areas of the Kasai, but was given options to buy land in a total area covering half of the Congo. This deadly joint collaboration began in 1906, with Leopold being granted half the profits from the companies. The American companies also had interests in Mexico and they prided themselves on treating their workers humanely and paying them a living wage. A company spokesman said that the same policy would also apply to the Congo for 'it was not good business to cut off a workman's hands or head'. It was after almost sixty years of association with the Belgians that the US monopoly combines, playing the role of junior partners, finally decided to push out the Belgians under the cover of the United Nations Organization.

One immediate result of the entry of monopoly capitalism during this phase was the dispossession of the peasantry from their land. Out of a total of 234 million hectares, 27 million were handed over to these giant monopolies, white settler plantation owners and mission stations. Further ex-propriation was through the establishment of a national park system which covered another 4 million hectares. The two provinces particularly affected were Kivu and Northern Katanga. After World War II, this dispossession of the peasantry was accelerated and white settlers came to the Congo in their hundreds. They were given farms of up to 500 hectares. Only beyond this figure was it necessary to obtain consent from the authorities. The demands of the companies and the white settlers for more land grew in in-tensity and were insatiable. The administration was under pressure both from individual settlers and large companies to make available substantial new land concessions for coffee in the north east, oil palm and rubber in the forest zones and extensive cattle ranching in the south.

The amount of 27 million hectares of the richest and most fertile land is high even for standards in a colonized country. It resulted in critical land shortage reaching explosive pro-portions in the provinces of the lower Congo, Kwilu, Kivu and parts of Katanga.

The Congolese peasant was enmeshed in the cotton econ-omy as early as 1917 when an ordinance was introduced which compelled the peasants to produce this cash crop. In 1932, 23,000 tons were produced, but by 1939 this reached the staggering total of 127,200 tons. In fact at one stage it appeared that the whole administrative machinery was geared to mobilize the peasants in this direction. Bureaucrats thus became agents whose job it was to coerce the peasant to produce his quota of cotton. It is small wonder then that the

agricultural officer, once regarded as an insignificant func-
tionary, shot up in importance in the Congo. At first the
decree of 1933 stipulated a maximum of 60 days compulsory
labour in the farms. After World War II it went up to 120
days, but observers noted that in practice the peasant had to
work continuously throughout the year. Two factors contributed to the ruin and dispossession of the cotton farmer.
In the years 1929–32 the dollar crisis in the US transmitted
shocks into the Congo as it did into other capitalist economies. The big monopolies operating in the Congo as well as
the trading cartels were hit by this crisis, and to save themselves put the Congolese peasants in the front line to absorb
these shocks. The effect of this was that the peasant was
forced to grow cotton, but now was paid next to nothing for
his produce. An observer then noted that such was the plight
and distress that an entire family had to work two or three
months to pay for the compulsory head tax.

It was the amount of tax payment that brought about the
ruin of the farmer. In 1957 for instance, he was paid six
francs per kilo and his average revenue was little more than
a thousand francs. But the Belgian franc has been gradually
losing its purchasing power as may be seen by the following
table:

Year	Value of franc
1914	1·0
1919–23	0·25
1924–5	0·20
1926	0·16
1927	0·13
1945–47	0·03

In other words, if one took 1914 as the starting point the
franc was worth only 3 per cent of its value. To put it
differently, the Congolese peasant engaged in cotton production was being robbed and ruined through inflation. The
land which he tilled had become a millstone round his neck.
What made it even more intolerable was the fact that even
the six francs was not always paid. The price fluctuated violently depending on the profits of the cotton manufacturing

companies, and the local marketing Boards. The latter before it paid the price to the peasant deducted operating costs, profits and overheads. If for instance the costs were high and profits poor, the peasants had to pay by being given a reduced price for their product.

The Congolese regarded forced cultivation of cotton as a price they had to pay for their oppression. They themselves saw no benefit from this system of hard labour. Thousands thus left their land and disappeared to reappear in the urban areas.

Details are not available for the low yield cotton-producing areas like north Katanga and Orientale Province, but it could be safely said that rural exodus took place in these areas as well. The expropriation of the peasantry and their flight from the land was a result of capitalist forces. The peasant left the land because he was ruined.

Although enmeshed in the capitalist system and a part of it, nevertheless the Congolese peasant and worker was subjected to a political administrative system that turned him into a serf or wage slave. A feature of the feudal relationship of production was that the serf had to give part of his labour to his lord without pay. This was also forced on the Congolese peasantry and was intensely resented. A contemporary observer noted that what annoyed the villager of the region most were the corvées to which they were subjected. The most striking of these were the obligation to transport (by hammock) any person black or white travelling in the name of the State, and his baggage, or execute tasks such as the repair of roads, and the construction and maintenance of houses for colonial agents. For those who complained it was prison. An administrator observed that the administrators were in a position to know that exactions were becoming more numerous every day and that they no longer left the population respite or liberty. They daily became more and more merchants of men, and villages emptied at their approach as at the approach of the slave trader.

Compulsory cultivation of the land, theoretically for 120 days, in practice amounted to tilling practically the whole year round. What this meant was that the peasant was tied to the soil. The Congolese peasant was thus turned into a serf.

The whole Belgian administrative system he thus saw as onerous and oppressive. It was through this administrative system that he was forced to perform compulsory labour in the cotton fields, and was subjected to the corvée. It was to this administrator that he had to pay the hated tax that took away what little he managed to save. He was forced to carry passes as well as give information to the census people, whom he regarded as spies. He thus turned against his oppressor and exploiter who offered him and his family no hope or future.

The whole capitalist system has been founded on the ownership of private property. This is considered as sacred as any of the ten commandments. A contradiction in Congolese society was that white imperialist conquest brought the Congolese within the capitalist relationship of production, yet they were denied the right to the ownership of private property or land. If there was one single issue that united the Congolese population, of peasants, workers and the petty bourgeoisie, intelligentsia and merchants, it was this demand of the right to own land. As early as 1946, Kasavubu alarmed the Belgians when he publicly raised the issue when he called for the restoration of land, referring to it as 'the right of the first occupant'. As a result of increasing pressure the Belgians enacted, on 10 February 1953, a decree which authorized private ownership of land by the Congolese. But this decree remained a dead letter, for the top bureaucracy, which consisted entirely of Belgians, just 'did not find the time' to implement it. In 1959, Lumumba raising this issue remarked: 'It is now four years since this Decree was promulgated and it has still not been effectively implemented. Congolese evolués and African settlers who wish to become owners of the land on which they have built property or durable materials, come up against all kinds of obstacles.'[4] Lumumba estimated that during this period out of a population of 12 million not more than five people in Leopoldville (Congo Kinshasa), and Elizabethville (Lumumbashi) were able to acquire title deeds to the land.

Applications were made to private organizations for loans to mortgage their property, some of which cost 300,000 francs. Applicants were told that the granting of loans was subject to the registration of their property, with the Conservaion des Titres Fonciers (Land Registry). When they applied to this Department to have their property registered, purely an administrative formality, they were told to wait, and that shortage of staff prevented the administration from giving active consideration to local measures for implementing the Decree.

While the Congolese were all united on the question of private ownership of land, just how it should be acquired brought about differences, for the different classes had different approaches. Concretely, this boiled down to the question whether it should be purchased from the State or not. Lumumba had graduated to become an evolué, but he was one of the few who kept his fingers on the pulse of the people as a whole. He went to the workers and peasants to find out what they felt and thought of the matter. He wrote: 'I have carried out a wide-ranging enquiry amongst different strata of the population to find out their views on land ownership, and especially on the purchase of land. After questioning native chiefs, various members of the working classes and the intelligentsia, I can roughly summarize their views as follows: The Congo is our common patrimony. The Europians came to civilize us and not to usurp the natural and inalienable rights bequeathed to us by our ancestors. These rights have always belonged to us *collectively*. If it is a case of replacing the system of communally-held property by the system of individual ownership, it is obviously fair to *share proportionally* the patrimony which belonged to us collectively, in such a way that each member of the community receives his share. This share, which belongs by right to each inhabitant, should be registered in the name of each family ... There can be no question of sale. Our forebears never *bought* land to cultivate their fields and build their houses ... we are poor and we have not the necessary money to buy this land. The Whites have taken hold of our rights – our lands – and now wish to sell them to us for money, as if we were strangers in the country. They have become owners of our land and we, the natives, have bcome mere immigrants, because our own land is now to be sold to us. . . . There is no objection if the State sells the land to native traders, because they have the means to buy it and they will get their money back in due course. But to sell the land to poor natives is unjust.'[5]

The peasant involved in cotton cultivation did not own more than half a hectare. This could apply to other peasants as well. The Congolese thus consisted of a nation of small peasants. It was their demands that Lumumba was expressing when he said that if private ownership of land was introduced it should be given to the peasant without payment, for apart from the fact that they had the right to it, there was the practical question. They had no money to buy the land.

Lumumba did not yet understand that capitalism is not in a position to implement that kind of agrarian reform. In fact, only socialists are in a position to carry out the demand of the poor and landless peasants of ownership of land without payment. In this sense already their national movement, with this basic demand of the peasant, was becoming part of the socialist revolution.

Lumumba urged the Belgian Government to implement this cry of 'land to the tiller'. But this was unrealistic, for it represented the most revolutionary of all the demands in the programme of any national movement. For its implementation would bring about a fundamental change of social relations. Neither imperialism, nor the bourgeoisie which has taken power, has been able to carry this out. But the realization of this demand gives the real democratic contact to the national movements for only with its implementation can the aspirations of the peasantry, the majority in a colonial country, be satisfied.

After the achievement of independence a few national movements have been able to carry this out. But by and large, the granting of political independence did not lead to the confiscation of the land of large plantation owners, or the mining monopolies, which have large tracts of land. The system of landholding has continued, as under the colonial masters, the only difference being that Africans with money can now buy land.

What Lumumba said of the Congolese peasantry applied to the peasantry of Africa in general. They are poor and lack the means to buy the land. If before independence all classes were united, now with freedom, there is separation precisely because a tiny section with wealth has been able to acquire land, while the masses remain landless as before, and still cannot acquire title deeds. The acquisition of land by a tiny section of the African wealthy class places it in the same camp as foreign settlers and monopolist combines. The basis of their unity is that they both own private property in land, against the mass of the peasants who are landless. The unfolding of the class struggle in Africa has as its battle arena the struggle for the land.

The bourgeoisie which took power at independence has proved itself utterly incapable of solving this burning problem of the people, because of its ties with imperialism. This then will fall on the shoulders of the socialist revolutionaries to push the struggle to its uppermost limit by fighting to realize the aspirations of the peasantry. The struggle will push new forces to the fore and thus accelerate the movement towards socialism.

3

CONGOLESE BOURGEOISIE

After World War II, imperialism recognized that it had to face two formidable and antagonistic forces. On the one hand it had to contend with the sharpening class struggle at home by its radicalized working class, and on the other hand an equally intense form of class struggle taking the character of a revolt of the submerged colonial masses of Asia and Africa. Its dilemma in the colonies was how to continue its policies of exploitation under new conditions. It was faced with two alternatives. It could mobilize the nation's resources and launch counter attacks of suppression and repression as it had done so ruthlessly in the past. On the other hand, it could make an appearance of physical withdrawal by the granting of political independence.

The far-sighted section of imperialists has realized that it was not possible to hold down the rapidly awaking masses of the colonial world. World War II had so weakened them that few could stand on their own feet, let alone afford the luxury of costly campaigns of suppression and annihilation. In any event such a course could very well give rise to a section within the national movement which would not only want to remove oppression, but also the entire economic system of exploitation.

Imperialism then appeared to change course and decided to withdraw physically. This saw a change in strategy. It threw away its well known blood-spattered garments characterizing its colonial rule, and now donned the garb of liberator. Imperialism announced that it was prepared to grant political independence.

It had calculated naïvely that by offering political freedom on a plate, it would in fact retain economic control and be able to intensify the system of exploitation. But to do that it had to forge an important link with the African bourgeoisie, who were expected to be its foremen, managers and if need be soldiers and policemen.

What is the nature of the African bourgeoisie? What are its constituent elements, its links and aspirations? Further, what is its direction of development? How is it that after being granted political control in some cases for almost ten years, it has proved itself totally incapable of solving the basic needs of the workers, and peasants? It has been surprising that although there has been a proliferation of books on African culture, African poetry and prose, no serious analysis has until very recently, been made of the African bourgeoisie. In this respect, Kwame Nkrumah's book *Class Struggle in Africa* is significant for in this pioneering work he attempts to analyse the composition of the African bourgeoisie. He writes: 'Africa has in fact in its midst a hard core

42

of bourgeoisie who are analogous to colonialists and settlers in that they live in positions of privilege – a small, selfish, money-minded, reactionary minority amongst vast masses of exploited and oppressed people. ... Their survival depends on foreign support.'[6] In this respect, the African bourgeoisie has much in common with the comprador class in China before the Revolution A comprador in the original sense of the word was a Chinese manager or a senior Chinese employee in foreign commercial establishments. A comprador, whether Chinese or African, has this in common – he is an appendage of the international bourgeoisie and serves their interests in the former colony or neo-colony.

Nkrumah in *Class Struggle in Africa*, classifies the various sub-sections of this class. It includes the national bourgeoisie and represents capitalism. These are traders, tradesmen, top civil servants, compradors (managers or senior employees of foreign enterprises), the professional and managerial 'class'. The petty bourgeoisie consists of farmers (rural petty bourgeoisie owning land and employing labour) and urban petty bourgeoisie (small traders, merchants and craftsmen). The bourgeois élites are intellectuals, top bureaucrats, the officer 'class' in the armed forces, professionals (top lawyers and doctors, etc.) and technocrats.

This examination of the bourgeoisie led Nkrumah to make this pointed comment: 'There was a marked absence of capitalists among the bourgeoisie since local business enterprise was on the whole discouraged by the colonial power. Anyone wishing to achieve wealth and status under colonialism was therefore likely to choose a career in the professions, the civil service or the armed forces, because there were so few business opportunities. Foreigners controlled mining, industrial enterprises, banks, wholesale trade and large-scale farming. In most of Africa the bourgeoisie was, in fact, for the most part petty bourgeoisie.'[7]

Engels described the bourgeoisie as the class of modern capitalist owners of the means of social production, and employers of wage labour. This was the bourgeoisie after almost five centuries of development in Western Europe, and refers to the dominant section of the bourgeoisie, namely the

43

industrial bourgeoisie. From this definition then, Nkrumah's characterization of the African bourgeoisie as a petty bourgeoisie is correct, for it does not control the means of production.

The decision by the major colonial powers to grant independence as embodied in the UN resolution to decolonize after World War II took Belgium unawares. However they were reassured and became reconciled when it was decided that the decolonizing process would be evolutionary and would extend over thirty years. Power was to be handed over to the evolués, the Congolese bourgeoisie, for the Belgians saw in them a class that would be able to save the capitalist system and maintain the economic interests of Belgium. But in fact there was no real bourgeoisie, since the growth of the entire people was stunted, and it therefore became official Belgium policy to create a bourgeoisie.

In Tanzania too it was the same. The International Bank of Reconstruction and Development said in its report in 1960 that it did not expect to see the emergence of an African bourgeoisie at least for the next ten years. It however added, 'The emergence of an African business community will necessarily be a gradual process ... (it will come) from the participation of Africans in commerce, success as settled farmers, and as artisans and technicians in industry. This would form the nucleus of the business community'. In other words, there was to be no independent growth of the African bourgeoisie. From birth it would be under the guardianship and tutelage of the imperialist masters.

The European settlers, a community normally the most reactionary, however, gave support to the proposals of the Belgian Government. Its mouthpiece, FEDACOL (La Federation Congolese de Classes Moyen), in a secret memoranda of 1955 to the colonial ministers stated: 'We must organize a class of evolué natives who will declare their acceptance of the ideals and principles of our Western civilization, and who will be our equals in rights and duties, less numerous than the native mass, but powerful and influential. They will be the allies it is indispensable to find in the native communities. These middle classes will be the black bourgeoisie which is beginning to develop everywhere, which we must help to enrich itself, and organize itself, and which like the bourgeoisie all over the world will be opposed to any disruption, internal or external.'[8]

Key to all this, however, was the right of the Africans to buy land, which though legally decreed, was never implemented. The Belgian Government in 1954 had launched a Congolese FEDACOL, called the Association de Classes Moyen Africain (ACMAF). The Congolese were now given facilities to study abroad, particularly in Belgium. Attempts were made by liberal Belgian intellectuals to cut across colour barriers and to have joint discussions with their Congolese counterparts. Lumumba belonged to such discussion groups and he himself acknowledged the important part they played in shaping his ideas in the early period. In 1958 Lumumba was the Vice-President of Amicale Liberal de Leopoldville and also joined a study group, the Centre et de Recherches Sociale (CERS) established by Jacques Meert.

In the evolués may be seen the emergence of the Congolese bourgeoisie. While it showed the same broad characteristics of its African counterpart, it also showed some distinct particularities. The distinctiveness lay not so much in the character of its composition but rather in its origins, and the overwhelming preponderance of the bureaucratic section over the rest.

The Belgians divided the Congolese successively into two, then three or four, new classes. In effect, at the beginning of the colonization period there were on the one hand the 'basond' (slang for uncivilized), and on the other hand the soldiers of the Force Publique. The soldiers (Congolese) had as their noble mission, the conquest of the regions inhabited by the Basondi, and their subjugation to the authority of the white man. A new class then appeared, that of 'boys', native domestic servants of the colonizers. The Belgians used them to consolidate their authority over the country. At the beginning of the era baptized 'Pax Belgica', the prestige of the domestic exceeded that of the soldier. They became catechists and taught the catholic religion, principal source of general pacification of the Congo by the colonizers. As the children of the 'boys' and soldiers went to school a new class grew up, that of evolués.

The immediate ancestor of the evolué was the soldier and the priest. The Catholic Church dominated the entire social and cultural life of the Congolese. Just as the peasant could not escape the administrator and recruiting agent, he could not dodge the missionary. Mission stations dotted the entire countryside, and so numerous were they that at one stage the Congo alone harboured one-third of Africa's total number of priests.

The European bourgeoisie, having in its ancestry the runaway serfs, has had a long record of resistance against the forces of feudalism. But the ancestry of the Congolese bourgeoisie lies in the mercenary who sold himself to his conquerors, and allowed himself to be used as an instrument to subjugate his people.

A bourgeoisie rooted in industrial production could not rise because the large monopolist combines which dominated the Congolese economy would not allow its growth. Monopolies do not allow the growth of competition anywhere, in Belgium, England, France or the USA, and therefore the Congo was no exception. In fact the giant international monopoly arose directly as a result of swallowing smaller capitalist enterprises or ruining them, all over the world.

The Congolese did not present a problem, for being debarred from owning land privately they were shut off from a major source of primitive accumulation. In the field of major import and export trade there was little hope, for this was also in foreign hands, usually one of the subsidiaries of the foreign combines. Even in local trade, advancement was blocked by the entrenchment of Greek and Portuguese small traders. The Congolese who were able to amass wealth were few and far between. One of the well known figures was Moise Tshombe's father. He had a financial empire with property, and a fleet of buses. It was his spendthrift son who crashed this empire, rendering him bankrupt. It was then that the son, Moise, graduated to politics. Then there were individuals like Victor Nendeka. He was the head of the dreaded Sureté. He owned a bar, a travel agency and an insurance company.

In fact to be classified as an evolué in the pre-independence era in the Congo one had to be economically independent, if not employed by the State or by a company. However, the bulk of the evolués were in employment, in administrative positions. Hardly anyone employed labour. The table shows the following position:[9]

Province	Planters	Artisans	Traders	Small businessmen	Professionals
Leopoldville	1,104	2,582	4,559	605	28
Equator	51	19	161	25	—
Orientale	252	90	1,774	188	—
Kivu	301	543	2,446	193	—
Katanga	53	112	2,067	101	1
Kasai	720	221	106	404	—

The bourgeoisie of the Communist Manifesto was the industrial bourgeoisie, which had revolutionized society from top to bottom. But the Congolese bourgeoisie was not only weak but a shadow of its European counterpart. In fact, the only way to change society in the Congo would be for a part of the petty bourgeoisie to break from their class and to cast its lot with the workers and peasants. This is just what Lumumba and Antoine Gizenga attempted to do when they set up their government in Stanleyville.

The classical bourgeoisie claimed the right to rule society and to take political power because it stood to end feudalism, eliminate backwardness, centralize government, and to develop the productive forces of society. Its own economic interests, coincided with this programme.

But the Congolese bourgeoisie, as elsewhere in Africa, is not the owner of the means of production. It is not even the owner of the instruments of production, like land. All these belong to the monopolies. It started off as a bourgeoisie without property, let alone capital. It is not rooted in the production or productive processes in society, and has no economic power. Hence it is in no position to revolutionize society, for the economic power is in the hands of the foreign super monopoly corporations.

The value of the economic resources of the Congo to international finance capital can be seen by the following table:

CONGO'S MAJOR EXPORT PRODUCTS 1958

Commodity	Tons	$m	% of World Output
Uranium	—	—	50
Copper	241,345	108	10
Oil palm products	235,762	50·5	30
Cotton	36,781	22·9	0·6
Coffee	70,603	56·3	2·0
Tin	2,580	8·3	9·0
Cobalt	9,701	22·5	75·0
Industrial diamonds	—	36·6	70·0
Gold	—	11·6	1·0
Metals*	441,197	3,500	—

* These include manganese, tantalite, tungsten and zinc

If there was chaos and confusion after Independence; if there was treachery and rank betrayal; if it led to the murder of Patrice Lumumba and a period of civil war, it was only because the stakes were very high as may be seen in the Congo's natural resources. If US imperialism worked feverishly to finance the UN operation; if it spent millions in corruption; if it worked ceaselessly to seat the Kasavubu delegation, it is only because it wanted to be certain that the government in power in the Congo was to be its mouthpiece.

The giant monopolies controlled what mattered. They decided what amount of surplus created by the sweat and toil of the workers should be consumed. It was they who decided firstly how much they must take for themselves, after grabbing the lion's share in the form of 'dividends to shareholders'. They decided how much the State was to be paid by way of taxation. The Congolese bourgeoisie in the government had to wait for the handouts from their economic lords. The payment is not direct, through taxation, but was payment all the same. It is this type of payment that transforms the bourgeoisie into the role of the foremen of imperialism. The fact that they hold posts as presidents ministers, MP's, heads of civil service, army and police officers does not conceal their essential role. They owe their positions to the real owners of the Congo's wealth the international bourgeoisie, and it is their function to serve these masters.

4

RISE OF THE CONGOLESE WORKING CLASS

THE capitalist relationship, with its mining, plantations and particularly the cotton economy engulfed the entire Congo, leaving little room for subsistence agriculture. The operations of the laws of capitalism resulted in the depopulation of the countryside, despite various legal and administrative measures to tie the peasant to the land. Lumumba recorded this tendency and laid the blame to some extent on the oppression and high-handedness of the chiefs. Urbanization proceeded rapidly after World War II, and some estimated that by 1960 Leopoldville had a population of 1·3 million people. On the eve of independence almost 25 per cent of the population lived on the land, and 37 per cent of the males had become wage earners. But 70 out of the total of 3,600 enterprises accounted for 50 per cent of the labour force. Of this, ten, headed by Union Minière, employed a total of one-fifth of the labour force.

A feature of this wage-earning class was that it was never completely proletarianized in that it never severed its roots completely from that of the peasantry, as was the case in

PERCENTAGE OF THOSE LIVING OUTSIDE
TRADITIONAL MILIEUX

Province	% of population	Province	% of population
Leopoldville	27·65	Kivu	19·03
Equator	21·62	Katanga	36·17
Orientale	23·02	Kasai	12·05

GROWTH OF THE MAJOR CITIES (IN THOUSANDS)

City	1945	1957
Leopoldville	96·0	370·0
Elizabethville	65·0	185·0
Stanleyville	20·0	78·0
Matadi	18·0	56·0
Coquihatville	12·0	33·0
Bukavu	4·5	34·0

GROWTH OF WAGE EARNERS (IN THOUSANDS)

Year	Wage Earners
1915	36·3
1925	274·3
1935	377·5
1945	701·1
1952	1,070·3

Europe. Apart from the administrative measures by the Belgians which made periodic raids to clean the urban areas of 'loafers', there was the economic factor. The wages paid to the workers, particularly those in the mines, were so low that they could not make ends meet. A capitalist pays a worker the minimum wage to keep him in a position to work the next day. But this wage covers food, clothing and housing for his wife and children as well. The South African mines, through the system of migratory labour, get out of paying this minimum by paying only for the worker himself. His family and his children have to fend for themselves in the reserves, that is on pieces of land far away from work. By this piece of robbery, the mine owners have amassed fortunes within a short space of time. What also helped was that the article produced was in general not consumed by the population so that the monopolist was not dependent on an internal market.

The Belgian monopolies however went one step further. Far from supporting the worker's family, the wages were so designed as to commit the family to partly suppporting the worker. Andre Boloko, a trade unionist, paints a moving picture of this ruthless system of exploitation, which has had few parallels in the world. He takes the town of Nioke as a representative one. It has a population of about 10,000. It has as its single major employer FORESCOM, a subsidiary of FORMINIÈRE, in turn a subsidiary of Société Générale. In 1956, most of the workers received 0.30 dollars a day with lodging provided by FORESCOM. Nearly 80 per cent of the married workers had cassava fields tilled by their wives. Some 67 per cent of them supplemented their income by fishing nearly every week-end. Somewhat surprisingly, most of the unskilled workers were dependent to an important degree on their families in the village. Some 70 per cent of them received packages from home two or three times a month. The enquiry found no cases of workers sending money back to the village.

The urbanization figures deal with only those who were legally allowed to be present in the cities. It does not mention the thousands of unemployed in the cities, particularly in cities like Leopoldville. But in January 1959, Leopoldville had at least a million people in the opinion of many observers. Many of them were young and had migrated to search for work and for better opportunities. In the towns they came into contact with political ideas. They took to Lumumba and those like him because they expressed their own desires. It was the workers and the unemployed who rose in revolt against the Belgian rulers on the 4 and 5 February 1959, seven days after Lumumba's mammoth rally. If there was one single incident that shook the nerves of the Belgian rulers and made them panic it was just this. They were never the same again. They began to give in, one after another, to the demands of the Congolese people.

Before the outbreak, observers noticed that there was a hostile mood on the part of the Congolese towards the Belgians. The latter were being jeered at and insulted as they passed in their cars. At the same time, the people organized spontaneously little meetings and began marching down the main streets and avenues.

The spark however that caused the explosion was the refusal of the authorities to allow Kasavubu's organization, the ABAKO (National Liberation Front) to hold a meeting. This angered the people, and the cry of independence heard from the lips of Lumumba a week earlier, was taken by the masses and made their own. Reports then of what took place conflict. Belgian official sources say that a police vehicle was set on fire, and that a band of men marched to the commercial quarter with the aim of sacking, looting and burning shops. During the nights of 4 and 5 January, public buildings, private residences, shops, social clubs, missions and stores were attacked in Leopoldville and the surrounding suburbs. Cars were set on fire and passers-by insulted. This report obviously whitewashes completely the ruthless and brutal measures adopted by the police and the army in suppressing what they believed to be a political insurrection. While admitting shooting by the police, the report says that it was all in self-defence.

However, a correspondent of an American newspaper gives a more correct picture of the barbarous acts of the rulers. He says: 'The government stepped in massively ... armouries were opened up and guns, along with thirty and forty rounds of ammunition, were issued to any European who presented himself at the door. In addition to arming themselves, the colonists formed themselves into voluntary platoons and regiments which took over the guarding of vital spots like oil dumps, and rail-road yards, while the regular army and police with armoured cars and mortar units took on the African townships themselves. ... For two nights, every African in the streets, individual or part of a mob was fired upon.'[10] Official figures state that 60 Congolese were shot dead, and that over 300 were injured. But the figures of both dead and injured were probably much higher.

A commission set up to enquire into the causes said that the political cause could be traced to 'foreign influence like the Accra Conference on the national movements'. One economic cause cited was unemployment, rising out of recession.

The government 'solved' the problem of unemployment in ways reminiscent of Nazi Germany and fascist South Africa. Its police conducted a house to house search and rounded up all those whom it considered were not gainfully employed, and whom it branded as agitators. Hundreds were detained and then packed off to the countryside to the areas where they had originally come from. In this way, the Leopoldville authorities boasted that they reduced unemployment in the city by 15,000.

These urban workers, many of them young men with some education went back to the homes of their fathers in the countryside without any wealth or property. Sometimes the clothes they had on was all they possessed. But they brought with them political dynamite – the idea of independence. They also carried with them the new thinking, that the Belgians were not omnipotent, and could be fought despite their superiority of weapons.

The countryside was seething with unrest, and what was lacking was a leadership with a programme that the people could grasp. The urban workers provided just this and in doing so they acted as catalysts. In such a political atmosphere, charged and tense, the people would gravitate round the organization which was the clearest and most unambiguous in interpreting their own demands. With Lumumba they found this clarity. Tribal and religious loyalties gave way as they now rallied to Lumumba and his organization. Unknown to the Belgian authorities, a mass movement was being born that would sweep the country.

5

MANIFESTO OF THE CONGOLESE BOURGEOISIE

THE Congolese bourgeoisie declared its programme, principles, methods of struggle, as well as organizational form through a document called the 'Manifesto de Conscience Africaine'. Published in 1956, it called for the establishment of a Mouvement Nationale Populaire, a movement of which Lumumba became the first President. This became known as the Mouvement Nationale Congolais (MNC).

The Manifesto proclaimed: 'We believe that there is a question of a 30-year plan for the political emancipation of the Congo ... we believe that such a plan has become a necessity if it is the intention to realize it in peace and concord ... this plan should express the sincere will of Belgium to lead the Congo to its complete political emancipation in a period of 30 years. Only an unequivocal declaration on this point will preserve the confidence of the Congolese towards Belgium.'

The background to the launching of the Manifesto was the publication by Professor A. A. Bilson in 1955 of a 'Thirty Year Plan for the political emancipation of Belgian Africa'. Representing the far-sighted section of the Belgian bourgeoisie he saw the dangers if no concrete proposals were made for political evolution of the Congolese, for as he said: 'If we wish it, our African territories will be in a position to take their proper destinies in their own hands. It is our duty and in our interest to see that this is done ... If we do not have a plan ... in 15 or 20 years, if not before, we will find ourselves faced by tensions and irresistible movements in several parts of our territories.'

In order to effect the political emancipation of the Congo, the Manifesto stated precisely how existing institutions could be transformed. The direction suggested could be two-

54

fold, for on the one hand, 'the existing institutions must become more and more representative by replacing progressively the present system of nomination with a system in which the population itself will designate its representatives ... on the other hand, the councils which are now purely consultative must receive true power of decision and control in increasingly extended matters in order to arrive finally at a responsible government at the head of our nation.'

The society it visualized for the Congolese people was to be purely a capitalist one. It was against any State participation in industry, and thus was even to the right of the Belgian Government. It plumped for the type of *laissez-faire* economy advocated by Adam Smith. It stated: 'Some people extol nationalization of large enterprises. We have no confidence in this capitalism of the State. Besides, are the workers in Europe much better paid and treated in nationalized enterprises than in private firms?' For the workers, however, it asked as a sop that minimum legal salaries which did not permit a decent life must be raised, and that there must be freedom to unionize. For the peasants it declared: 'For the mass of the population which remains in the villages, consideration must be given to the agricultural economy, village life must be made more agreeable – beginning by suppressing the loathsome system of forced cultivation.' It brought to the notice of the colonial masters that 'the middle classes are an important element in the economic and social life of the Congo'. Pleading for this group it said: 'An increasing number of Congolese want to take more responsibility and more initiative on the future of their country. They wish to assimilate in their national life other basic values of Western civilization, respect for the individual and for his fundamental liberties without racial distinction, a more intense pursuit of social justice, a true democracy based on equality of all men, and the participation of the people in the government of the country.'

It attacked racial discrimination and privilege based on colour, for it said: 'One principle is essential to us; the colour of the skin confers no privilege. To uphold privilege ... would be a source of conflict; we reject with vehemence the principle "Equal but separate". It is deeply offensive to us.' It called for the establishment of a broad national movement for 'we are convinced that it is wholly possible for pagans Catholics, Protestants, Salvationists, Mohammedans to agree on a programme of common good ... the Congolese can realize this programme most surely by being united. ... We are convinced that in the more or less future it will be necessary to give a more precise form to the ideas which we wish to promote, and there will have to be an organization'.

On the question of how these modest and reformist aims were to be realized the Manifesto stated: 'The organization which we anticipate would come into being in full legality conforming to the laws and regulations in force ... we have decided not to let ourselves be drawn into violence, because violence produces insoluble problems. We have only one aim, the good of the Congolese nation. We will make this aim triumphant in lawfulness and by peaceful means. Those who use violence show that they are not fit for true democracy.'

The basic demands of the Congolese bourgeoisie as stated in the Manifesto were the same as those put forward by the far-sighted section of the Belgian bourgeoisie. The identity of views in the political field was but a reflection of the growing class interests of the two. It has been the practice of the ruling classes, when faced with the revolt of an entire section of the people who are oppressed and exploited to detach itself from the establishment and to go and forge links with a certain layer of the oppressed. In this way it seeks to bring about a division in the national front.

The authors of the Manifesto were honest. They did not hide the fact that they were concerned with promoting the interests of their class, and the Manifesto said specifically it was addressed to the élite. What the bourgeoisie was asking was that it be trained as quickly as possible in the 30-year period, to be able to take over the functions of the State machinery. At the end of this period it visualized not complete independence but 'political emancipation'. In other words, it was begging that it be promoted as joint partners with the Belgians to administer the State machinery.

On two points the Manifesto makes it clear that it was not interested in tampering with the system in any way. Pandering to the Belgian bourgeoisie in a most shameless way it stated that it stood for the classical capitalism of a *laissez-faire* economy, which involved a minimum of State control, and certainly no state participation in the enterprises of the bourgeoisie. In other words, the Manifesto regarded the Belgian Government's involvement in economic enterprises in the Congo as too radical and also revolutionary. Not only then did it want the grip of the monopolies to continue, but it was prepared to hand over to the international bourgeoisie for pillage and plunder the State's economic interests in the Congo. They thereby stated before Independence that they would be willing to perform the roles of managers and foremen for international finance capital.

What gives a national movement its democratic content is its determination to solve the burning problem of the peasantry. Land hunger and onerous feudal relationships had turned the Congolese peasant into a serf. What is shocking about the Manifesto is that from all the outrageous system of exploitation and oppression which the Congolese peasantry suffered, the only improvement demanded in the Manifesto was the removal of the burden of forced cultivation. Lumumba at this stage held many ideas similar to those expounded in the Manifesto. But on the essential problem of land to the peasants it was clear he held fundamentally different views. He boldly stated that not only did the people want land, but that it should be given to them without payment. It is this that gave Lumumba's nationalism its democratic content.

The Belgian Government had already decreed that the Congolese should acquire private ownership of land, but so timid were the authors of the Manifesto that they did not even ask that this be implemented. The democratic essence of a national movement is the liberation of the peasants from their feudal fetters. The Manifesto's failure to incorporate the demands of the peasantry meant a national movement without democratic demands. The demands for the freedom of speech, of movement, of right to organize, and even of

57

universal franchise can only have validity when the majority of the people are freed from their serf-like positions under colonial oppression. What meaning can a vote have if the peasant cannot own land and is forced to perform the corvée?

The authors of the Manifesto revealed their true intentions when they stated that they aimed at 'liberal democracy'. What they said they wanted were the institutions of capitalist society, that is, parliament, a cabinet, a judiciary, and certain freedoms like that of the press. They also wanted visible symbols of colonial domination like colour discrimination to be abolished. They thus wanted a superstructure to be grafted on to Congolese society without altering its feudal relationships. This programme of liberal democracy is counter-posed against the programme of 'people's democracy' which seeks to solve the basic and fundamental problems of the mass of the people. The liberal programme of the Manifesto called for the elimination of racial discrimination, but remained silent on the crucial question of economic discrimination which had turned the peasant into a starving serf as a result of the seizure of land by the monopolists and plantation owners. The liberal programme of the Manifesto was aimed at solving the problems of a particular class only, namely the Congolese bourgeoisie. In fact, the authors had no intention of doing anything more than scratch at the surface for they said: 'The new Euro-African society we are building today must be administered and directed jointly by the Belgians and the Congolese.' The programme, the policy and its strategy of non-violence, show the class consciousness of the Congolese bourgeoisie, for what it was doing was to launch a reformist national movement with the end result of a partnership of the Congolese and Belgians for the continued exploitation of the people.

The organization of the Belgian settlers, the Fedacol, had suggested the creation of a Congolese middle class. While this was being evolved, its ideology, programme, policy, and framework within which it would operate was already being formulated by the Conscience Africaine and its Manifesto.

The significance of the Manifesto lay in its universality,

for it could well be applicable not only to Africa but also to Asia. The granting of political independence by the ruling colonial powers was designed to bring about a society of liberal democracy, that is democracy for the indigenous bourgeoisie to share in the exploitation of the masses.

The present period of struggle against imperialism for economic independence, also means a struggle against the indigenous bourgeoisie, particularly that section lodged in the State machinery and growing fat on the sweat and toil of the masses.

6

EVOLUÉ POLITICS

LUMUMBA did not take part in the drawing up of the Manifesto, for in this period he was in Stanleyville. However, he was in agreement with it on a number of points. He set forth his ideas in a remarkable book, the English version of which is titled: *Congo my Country*. He wrote this in 1956–57, while in Stanleyville, and in it one can see the same kind of thinking as that of the Manifesto group namely the liberal bourgeoisie nurtured by the colonial power and operating within the ranks of the Congolese nationalists.

The dominant ideas in any given period are those of the ruling class. It was the same in the Congo, and the ideas of the people which would rise to challenge these had still to be formulated. It is then not surprising that the most advanced ideas that the evolués held were those of the liberal Belgian bourgeoisie, for they had been denied contact with the revolutionary currents of the world. Since ideas do not drop from the skies, but are rooted in the concrete conditions of life, Lumumba took and made as his own what he believed were the most advanced ideas of his group. But the essential point was that his ideas were in a process of flux, and therefore what he wrote in his book was not final, or the last word on the matter. His book was published posthumously and had he lived it is very clear that he would either have refused its publication, or would have altered large sections of it.

The purpose of his book, published first in Belgium under the title *Congo, land of the future, is it threatened?* was in the words of the author: 'to make a contribution towards the search for a solution for the present and future problems of the Congo.'[12] With this in view he travelled throughout the Congo carrying out a study of some of the main social, economic and political problems affecting the everyday life of the people. 'My investigations have not been limited to the evolué class; they have also been carried out among the working class and the traditionalist leaders – the chiefs, nobles and others. I have established contact with people of all types and all shades of opinion. In consequence, I feel competent to summarize the various opinions which were expressed without going too wide of the mark.'[13]

In a letter to his publishers he wrote: 'I am self taught and I have never stopped learning. At present I am studying law, philosophy, economics, social science and administration. I am helped in this by European teachers who give their services free of charge.'[14]

At that time, Lumumba believed that every Congolese evolué should have a Belgian as his guardian: 'It seems to me that the best formula is that of personal relationship, which means that every Congolese who is aiming towards a certain ideal must make a serious effort to become more closely acquainted with a European with whom he is in contact. This European would be both his friend and mentor or his "sponsor". This kind of contact is better than group contacts on café terrace or occasional propaganda meetings.'[15] What Lumumba was suggesting was exactly what was in fact being done in many parts of colonial Africa where the leaders of national movements were being groomed by discreet and unofficial contacts with the liberal section of the ruling class.

Lumumba sent two letters to his publishers. The first dealt with why he wrote the book, while the latter gave some useful hints about his life: 'I am the founder-President of the Amicale des Postiers, (Post Office Workers' Friendly

Society). Since 1955, this association, which originally
catered only for native Post Office workers has included
European and Congolese officials in the postal services.

'After being Secretary of APIC (Association of Native
Public Servants) ... I was elected President in 1955 and I
still hold that office. In addition, I am a founder member of
the Committee of the Belgo-Congolese Union in Stanleyville, an inter-racial association which includes Belgians
and Congolese ... I am one of the first Congolese to be
granted Immatriculation and given equal status with Belgians. I was a member of the delegation of Congolese leaders
who visited Belgium in 1956 ... Apart from being chairman
of several cultural groups for Africans, I am a regular con-
tributor to several newspapers in the Congo and also to
L'Afrique et le Monde a Belgian newspaper published in
Belgium. In addition I am chief editor of the post office
journal *L'Echo* ... It was at my request that the Governor
General authorized me, by his decision issued in the official
Bulletin of the Belgian Congo, to publish this journal. I may,
therefore be ranked amongst the journalists editing newspapers in the Congo.'[16]

This letter was dated 2 February 1957. In the first one,
written a month earlier, he stated that his four primary aims
in writing the book were:

1. to convey the ideas and aspirations of the Congolese
   people on the various economic, social and political
   problems which are of particular concern to them, and
   on the solution of which – a happy solution, I hope –
   depend the future of the Congo and the success of Belgium's colonial mission;

2. to enlighten the Belgian authorities in particular and
   the colonists in general, as to the way in which the
   Africans in the Congo envisage their future in the
   world of today and tomorrow;

3. to give accurate, factual explanations of the reasons for
   the anxiety and discontent prevailing amongst the
   Congolese population;

4. to suggest to African political leaders certain reforms

which seem to me to be indispensable if the Belgians really wish to avoid a crisis and a loss of confidence among the African population whom they administer.[17]

Had Lumumba lived he would certainly have revised many of the chapters of his book, for by his actions, speeches, and the new political programme of his party there is little doubt that he had outgrown the ideas which he held before the Accra Conference of 1958. The world of the oppressed and exploited came to know Lumumba as a radical nationalist who refused to surrender his principles; and also as an anti-imperialist and a Pan-Africanist. His book shows him as a moderate nationalist and that was probably the reason why it was considered suitable for publication in the West.

There is no need for the followers of Lumumba and his admirers to be on the defensive on this score, and even less to try to hide his earlier views. Most of the leaders of independent African States today, and in those days those who headed the nationalist movements, held similar ideas to Lumumba in the 1955–57 period. Today, some of these leaders are in the forefront in the struggle for economic independence and are thus inviting the wrath of the former colonial masters. On the other hand, there are leaders who have not shifted from their views even after a decade of independence.

Lumumba outgrew his earlier ideas, and the resulting changes in his political and economic thinking may be seen in the context of a struggle between the old ideas of the dominant class, the Belgian bourgeoisie, and the ideas of the new and emerging force of Congolese peasants and workers. In this ideological struggle, honest and sincere nationalists had to choose which side to join for both the rulers and the people chose them and claimed them. In the end it was the people who were victorious for it was they whom Lumumba joined. He became the spokesman for the Congolese people, formulated their ideas and drew inspiration from them. On the question of land, already he was putting forward their ideas. With increased political consciousness, he took over and gave the people's demands political formulation. The privileged and propertied classes, both Belgian and Congolese, looked at him with hatred, for in their eyes, one of their own had left them to join the camp of the enemy. In short, Lumumba had become a traitor to his own class, the Congolese bourgeoisie. It is precisely because he had broken from his class, had cut his umbilical cord and plunged into the masses that he caught their imagination to become their idol and hero. The very people who groomed him now sought to destroy him.

In his book, Lumumba spoke for the élite, the evolués. It is their anxieties, their frustrations as well as their hopes and aspirations which he expressed. To his publishers he stated that his book was not final and that he planned more books. He did not live to be able to set down and formulate the aspirations of the workers and peasants whose interests he expressed, defended, and advanced in the last three years of his life.

The Manifesto had laid down in broad outlines, the programme, policy and the methods of struggle of the Congolese bourgeoisie. Lumumba gave these formulation, depth and concreteness, and he also projected clearly what type of society he would like to see emerge in the future. His canvas was wide and he proposed reforms in the prison system, the police, the civil service, the educational system, land tenure as well as what he called native institutions. He stood out against racialism; and the women of the Congo found in him their champion.

There are contradictions in his book. For instance in an earlier chapter he refers to the people as dull witted and illiterate, yet towards the end he urges his fellow evolués to keep the interests of the mass of the people in mind for our task 'is to concern ourselves not with a single class (evolués) but with the population as a whole'.[18] These are contradictions inherent in growth itself, for his ideas were developing and maturing. But in the book it may be seen that the direction of these ideas was unmistakable. Lumumba was moving away from the viewpoint of the rulers and was moving towards that of the people.

In the book, Lumumba pointed out to his masters that the evolués had an important role to play and could be very useful to the rulers. He wrote that the mass of the Congolese had an instinctive distrust of the white man. The result was that the rulers did not really know what the people were saying, doing and thinking. Secret organizations like the Kitawala, a politico-religious movement flourished in secret. The Belgians had tried for years to crush it and failed. Lumumba described his experience with the members of this sect: 'I approached some followers of the Kitawala sect and asked them some precise questions. My request was given short shrift, as they took me for an emissary of the Whites. Finally, after using much skill and diplomacy to prove to them that this was not the case, and that I was their 'blood brother' and could not betray them, they decided, with some hesitation, to reveal the mysteries of their sect.'[19] He carried out the investigation to show how important it was that the Congolese élite, who enjoyed the confidence of their fellow Congolese should work in close collaboration with the Belgians to enlighten them on certain questions.

He envisaged the Congolese middle class acting as a link between the Congolese people and the Belgian rulers. He said that their usefulness lay precisely in the fact that the Congolese masses trusted them, while they did not trust the Belgians. On the information provided by the evolués, the authorities would thus be able to deal with 'subversive elements', and be better able to carry out their policies.

Lumumba at that time envisaged the sharing of political power. He wrote that he believed it would be possible to grant political rights to the Congolese élite and to the Belgians of the Congo in accordance with certain criteria to be laid down by the Government, though there would be no question of granting these rights to people who were unfit to use them. He suggested that the *status quo* could be maintained for the uneducated masses who would continue to be governed and guided – as in all countries – by the responsible élite. But in this proposed partnership of oppression and exploitation, the role of the Congolese was to be that of a junior, very junior, partner. For the 'categories of Congolese to whom political rights could be granted if this should one day be possible (were to be):

- all those who are able to read and write, a fact which would have to be proved by the production of a certificate or of a document certifying that the person concerned has had a full primary education; such documents to be established in accordance with local regulations;
- chiefs, nobles and native judges (in the case of illiterates, the vote would be registered by a representative of the Government or by a jury formed for that purpose in each centre or commune). It would be bad policy to refuse the vote to native authorities, even if illiterate, unless the administration should decide otherwise.

'That would form the first transitional step towards universal suffrage, which would come with the introduction of universal education.'[20] The political integration would be able to take place side by side with legal integration. Lumumba wanted all the Congolese élite to be exempted from:

- restricted movement during the hours of darkness within the urban districts and European centres;
- imprisonment in the native district prisons;
- punishment by flogging in prison;
  (and to give them):
- 'the right to attend all cinema performances;
- the right to hold property (a privilege which is granted to all Congolese, immatriculés or not, under the Decree of 10 February 1953;
- unrestricted purchase and consumption of alcoholic beverages;
- hospitalization in European clinics (only for immatriculés).'[21]

Lumumba in the later years fought these very ideas which

he was then writing about. Their significance however lies in the fact that after a decade of independence, the reality is that in certain countries, there is still a determination to maintain the *'status quo* for the uneducated masses'. They are still governed and exploited by the responsible élite; the white and black élite. The only difference is that the white élite might be in London, Paris, Washington, Lisbon, Bonn or Brussels.

It has been possible to maintain the oppression of the masses through the introduction of universal suffrage. For with their financial resources, their links with backward and reactionary layers, through fraud, rigging, bribery and corruption coupled with open and naked teror against their opponents the African bourgeoisie have been able to ensure their election to power.

In the economic field Lumumba in those days expressed the generally-held view of the Belgian liberals that: 'The Europeans bring to the Congo their capital, their intelligence and their experience, whilst the natives supply their energy, muscle and labour power; the European supervises and directs, while the African works hard, loyally and willingly.'[22]

However Lumumba stated that from his investigation of the conditions, backed up with statistics, he came to the conclusion that the Congolese workers were poorly paid and suggested that the principle of equality in wages should be applied. Again however, he suggested that as a first step, where the efficiency of a Congolese worker was equal to that of a European, then his pay should be not less than three-quarters of the pay of a European of the same grade.

He listed the advantages of implementing the principle of equality

- 'It would go far towards eliminating the causes of tension and discontent amongst competent people who feel that they are victims of discrimination solely on account of the colour of their skins;
- it would prove to everyone that there is no question of racial discrimination but only of social discrimination,

66

which exists in every country in the world and is based mainly on the merits and aptitudes of the individual;
- it would rid certain Europeans, who are not fully aware of their role as educators, of a superiority complex in their relations with the Africans, a complex created not by the colour of their skin but simply and solely by their superior economic position;
- it would bring to the labour market a healthy competition which would act as a powerful spur to productivity and would benefit both employer and worker;
- it would spur on those who are discouraged and lazy;
- it would remove any doubt as to the sincerity of the policy of non-discrimination professed by Belgium, a doubt which exists (often wrongly) in the minds of quite a number of people;
- it would prove to all that the Belgo–Congolese community and the principle of the equality of its citizens is not an empty phrase but something which is steadily being put into practice;
- it would firmly rebut the cynical allegations which certain people tend to put forward to the effect that the Government's policy is a policy of talk and half measures; allegations which are intended to sow confusion in the minds of the Congolese and discredit Belgian achievements in Africa;
- it would facilitate a speedier integration of the native élite;
- finally, it would strengthen trust, understanding and solidarity between Belgians and Congolese and thereby increase the authority of the Government.'[23]

Lumumba observed that there were two legal systems operating in the Congo, one for the Europeans and the other for the Congolese. In the former, if the offender happened to be convicted, then he would be either fined or have a suspended sentence. In the latter it would be the maximum sentence, usually involving a period of long imprisonment. Here then was there not only a different system for white and black, but also one based on class, with the workers and peasants, who were Congolese, receiving the heavy hand of the State and its whiplash.

He recalled that imprisonment for a long time was foreign to traditional African society and that before the arrival of the European, no one had ever been detained in prison for a period of years, or for the whole of his life. Offenders were usually punished quickly. The Congolese had never known the outbreaks of offences which were then prevalent in the Congo. Theft, for instance, was rare before the arrival of the Europeans. You could close your house with a piece of string and go off on a journey lasting several weeks without fear of anyone breaking in.

His chief criticism of the penal system was that it did nothing to reform the prisoner. Rather the opposite was the case, for it was in prison that the person was exposed to harmful influences which affected them for the rest of their lives.

The food in prisons was so bad that it was practically uneatable. They were forbidden to wear vests, pants or shoes, unless a special permit was supplied by the doctor. They slept on boards, laid on the ground. Urging the amelioration of prison conditions rather than any drastic reform Lumumba said that the Congolese did not wish to live in luxury, but wanted to serve their sentence under better conditions. A prison is always a prison, a place for punishment. However, Lumumba believed that there should be a change in the penal system so that prisoners should be able to live in more humane conditions more in keeping with human dignity.

There are still African governments debating whether corporal punishment should be abolished or retained. Lumumba on this score was quite categorical. He said that it was time that flogging was abolished as a punishment in the Congo. This primitive punishment was a relic which was no longer appropriate in the present circumstances. In the nineteen-fifties this question excited much heat and discussion, and Lumumba quoted the view of the advocates who said: 'If flogging is abolished that will be the end of discipline among the natives; they will no longer stand in awe of the

Europeans and the representatives of authority, there will be disorder.'[24] Lumumba answered this argument with a biting attack showing the Lumumba of the future. He said: 'I do not believe that the whip is the reason why the Congolese have so far remained attached to the Belgians; it is not because of the whip that the Congo has been built up; it is not because of the whip that native workers come and offer their services to the European; it is not because of the whip that these large and flourishing plantations and the colossal enterprises which are scattered all over the Congo have enriched their owners; it is not because of the whip that the Belgo–Congolese Community will be built up, but through mutual esteem and trust.'[25] Lumumba in this condemnation of the use of the whip showed clearly to any discerning reader that he was wide awake and knew what had taken place, and what was taking place.

In his book, Lumumba states that the prison authorities were a law unto themselves, for although Circular No. 1 Just. dated 31/8/1947, specifically excluded certain categories of Congolese, such as the clergy, evolué officials, NCO's in the Force Publique from being flogged, the instruction was ignored.

The State, according to Lumumba, is an instrument of coercion and suppression and this is impressed on the people daily through the actions of the policemen in a colonial society. Police brutality, police arrogance, police extortion is a phenomenon found in all exploitative and oppressive societies where the protection of private property has become more important than the saving of lives. The Congo was no exception and Lumumba remarked that the majority of policemen had no clear conception of what their job involved; instead of the police being servants of the public and adopting a courteous attitude to members of the public, it was the public who were in the service of the police and often witnessed regrettable scenes between police and citizens.

He suggested short term reforms, and one was the discontinuance of recruitment of illiterate policemen. He said that the only way to secure educated and competent policemen was to make the policeman's career more remunerative; otherwise there would always be second-rate people enrolling in the police force as a last resort, like despairing men enrolling in the Foreign Legion.

On the question of racialism, or as Lumumba put it, 'The Clash between White and Black' he declared that the cause was primarily economic and social, and continued: 'When the "economically strong" wish to enjoy a higher standard of living and earn more at the expense of others, the latter – i.e., the proletariat – revolt against the capitalists and the bourgeoisie, thus producing a clash of interests.

'The struggle of the poor against the rich is a continuous process which is evident in all human groups and has nothing to do with race. These tendencies can be seen even amongst people belonging to the same race ... This is an inherent tendency in human nature: man's selfishness and his inclination to exploit his fellow-man.'[26]

Many of the leaders of the national movement become infected with the racialism of the ruling class. Their own inverted racialism takes the form of considering all Europeans as oppressors and exploiters. Lumumba was free from this insidious disease just as he was also free from tribalism. But although he recognized the existence of racialism, he believed that the majority of the Belgians in their hearts did not harbour racial feelings. Racialism on their part, stemmed from what he described as the colonial attitude of mind, for it is 'the quite natural desire of any person in a privileged position to preserve a certain distance, economic and social, between himself and persons of an inferior rank'.[27] Above all, Lumumba saw the interdependence of the two groups in the Congo, for, as he said, the Blacks would be helpless without the Whites and the Whites would be helpless without the Blacks.

Lumumba was free from racialism largely because he came into contact with Europeans through multi-racial associations. He was a founder member of one in Stanleyville. He observed that at such meetings racialism could be sensed at the tip of certain tongues, European as well as Congolese. However he felt that these multi-racial associations, if properly directed, could play a valuable part in the sphere of human relations. He considered that the main purpose of inter-racial groups should be to provide social and civic education to both Europeans and Africans.

Lumumba's non-racialism was put to a severe test a few years later. With Independence, Lumumba became identified with the revolutionary nationalist leaders who also were strongly anti-imperialist. The Belgian ex-rulers promoted a smear campaign against him in order to discredit him. He was called a 'barbarian' and his followers 'primitive savages'. Lumumba fought back with vigour and determination, and exposed the machinations of the former colonial power and asked that they leave. But at the height of this controversy, never did he stoop to racialism, for at that very time he appealed to the Belgian teachers to remain to help his government in uplifting the Congolese people. He thus drew a distinction between the Belgian oppressors and the Belgian people.

His nationalism then was one which was free from the virus of racialism. He said that it was necessary to avoid false nationalism which concealed forms of racialism and hatred for those of another race. This kind of nationalism whether among Congolese or Europeans, must be combated because it gives rise to racial hatred.

The nationalism of Lumumba aimed at creating a nation state out of the Congo, where everyone, black and white, where every member of every tribe would be treated as equal citizens provided they owed their loyalty to the country and by labour contributed to the prosperity of the country. This is the Congo he wished to see arise, and it is this cherished dream of his that was not realized in his lifetime.

Lumumba had an outstanding quality which is necessary in a leader. He was totally involved in the people, even when he personally did not espouse their particular cause. He then would present their point of view and leave it at that. If he was a rapid talker, he was a great listener and a shrewd observer. Some of the finest passages in his book occur when he records conscientiously what the people felt about the burning issues of the day like that of land, freedom of movement, or the police.

He began his book, facing the Belgian rulers and writing mainly what would please them. When the views of the people were presented he would add his little comment so as not to be misunderstood. But in the latter part of the book one sees the shift in his position. He then referred to the Congolese as 'Africans' and not 'natives'. He showed evidence of the political maturity of the Congolese people and did not add his own comments. Thus in the *Conclusion – Crisis of Confidence* he wrote: 'In their co-existence with the Whites, the Africans are greatly worried, not by the fact of living alongside them, but by the idea that they may never be able to attain complete emancipation whilst under European domination. Hence the Afircan's dream of independence does not arise from the hatred for the Whites or a desire to drive them out of Africa but simply from the wish to be not merely a free man, but also a citizen in the service of his country and not perpetually in the service of the European. He believes, moreover, that even if he is able to obtain complete emancipation under white domination it will only come after centuries, because the European will hamper that emancipation by all sorts of tricks and political schemes and that the Blacks will therefore be kept in a state of inferiority as long as possible. Finally, he believes that once the country becomes independent, the emancipation of the inhabitants will be much more rapid than it would have been under the system of tutelage and colonialism.'[28]

And in a searing indictment of Belgian imperialism he stated: 'Since the European occupation began, some eighty years ago, no African in the Congo has been accepted for any post – even the lowest – of European officer grade in the administrative services, the law and the army, even if he has had a full secondary education and studied philosophy for several years. ... A European (I refer here to temporary officials some of whom have had no secondary education), is *always* superior to an African even if the latter has studied longer and hence is better educated.'[29]

And if there was tension in the Congo, resulting in a crisis of confidence, he put the blame fairly and squarely on the shoulders of the rulers. 'Much has been said recently about the "crisis of confidence". I must say frankly that this crisis is the inevitable consequence of broken promises, of past faults, of the *unjustified* perpetuation of certain discriminatory measures.... These ... are the sole source of the crisis and of all its potential consequences.'[30]

Revealing that the curtain by which the Belgians had sealed off the Congo from the main streams of world civilization was now falling into shreds he said that the evolués read, discussed and were fully aware of everything which went on in the world. They took an increasing interest in political life. They were not unaware of the movements which were growing up in the other African colonies, where their neighbours were demanding autonomy and independence. They envied the position of some colonies and wanted to secure a similar position in their turn.

He told the rulers rather bluntly that the rise of the national movement was inevitable and it would be the height of folly to suppress it. Even if the Security Service was doubled and watch was kept on all characters suspected of nationalist tendencies, it would be pointless, for even if every Congolese was kept under surveillance by a police officer, even if the Congo was surrounded by iron bars, emotions and thoughts could not be suppressed. Lumumba was heralding the rise of the nationalist movement which come what may, could not be crushed, however mighty the colonial power.

7

WOMEN IN CONGOLESE SOCIETY

ONE of the tests of any revolutionary leader is his attitude towards class, race, colour and sex. The leaders of the nationalist movement in Africa either came from, or were connected with polygamous households. And nowhere was the position of women in society so depressed and debased as in a polygamous household in the colonial era. The woman there was compelled to carry many burdens. Like the male counterpart she suffered national oppression and class exploitation; and also in the household she was oppressed because of her sex.

Leaders of national movements sometimes adopted very contradictory positions. On the one hand they fought bravely and heroically to end colonial oppression and exploitation, and one of their strongest demands was to end discrimination and inequality based on colour. Yet these very leaders then practised discrimination and inequality when it came to their daughters and wives at home, even believing that the political fight to end oppression was solely to be a man's affair. They believed that it was possible to construct a modern and healthy society with a polygamous household as the family unit.

Lumumba felt strongly and deeply at the debasement and degradation of women. He realized that they had become mere chattels who existed to satisfy the whims and pleasures of the male overlord. In fact, it is in the chapter on women, in his book *Congo My Country*, where one discerns the Lumumba of the later period as one capable of feeling intensely and passionately about injustices all around him. His noble feelings were outraged at the way the repression of women was dehumanizing and brutalizing them. If Lumumba could speak out strongly and openly on this score it was because here was a sphere which did not touch directly the colonial administration nor the Belgian bourgeoisie. His criticism is levelled against the Congolese élite whom he believed ought to behave better because of their education. In one of his passages he gives a moving and vivid picture of the wife's harassment, and the conceit and the despotism of the Congolese male. 'When the boss wants to have water on the table, instead of going to get it himself – even when it is within reach of his hand or only three yards away from the dining-table – he barks to his wife "Marie, mai (Marie water!)" even when Marie, completely worn out by exhausting work (going to the market which may be several miles away, looking after the children single-handed, doing the

regarded the narrow outlook of the Roman Catholic Church. 'Here is the argument used by parents in the villages: "Of what use is it for a girl to go to school if she cannot afterwards work in an office to earn money? We do not want to send our children to the Sisters because, once they are baptized, they will be compelled to enter into 'chapel marriages' (that is, religious marriages); then they will be regarded as 'slaves' because, even if they are ill-treated by their husbands they will no longer be able to leave them in order to marry another man. We should be selling our daughters if we allowed them to go to the Mission in order to enter into that kind of marriage" '.[35]

The tribal customs of the people of the Congo are actually far more humane and generous to the woman than the backward, narrow and archaic practices of the Roman Catholic Church which condemns married women to life-long bondage and suffering. Congolese traditional society left the woman with a choice. Instead of ruining her whole life with a husband who was temperamentally incompatible, she was given the choice of leaving him. And when she did, it was with the sanction of the whole of society. There is little doubt that had Lumumba given this matter further thought, particularly after independence, he would have swept away this archaic notion of the indissolubility of marriage.

Lumumba was head and shoulders above his contemporaries in his attitude towards women. In this he was thoroughly modern, for he desired their emancipation so that they would be able to play their rightful role in society. But he did not completely realize their potentialities as a political force, whose creative energies locked up for centuries, once released, could be a mighty force in revolutionizing society. But then this would have come with the growth of consciousness of the national movement. However, in his own way, he paid the Congolese women the greatest tribute that they could have wished for, because his last political testament, when he knew that he was about to die was written to a woman – his wife Pauline.

77

8

THE ALL-AFRICAN PEOPLES'
CONFERENCE, ACCRA 1958

By the middle of 1958, the political climate of Africa showed a distinct change. Ghana, under the leadership of Kwame Nkrumah, had achieved its independence in 1957 and de Gaulle, the President of France, had proclaimed from Congo Brazzaville within hearing distance of Leopoldville, that as far as he was concerned anyone who desired independence could have it. This was taken note of in Belgium, and it had an effect also on the evolués of Leopoldville. The anachronistic régime of the Congo was denounced, and the MNC intellectuals now redefined their positions. They urged the rapid democratization of existing consultative institutions; the immediate acquisition of fundamental liberties, consistent with the Charter of the United Nations; and the liberation of the Congo from the shackles of imperialism. But all these aims would, they hoped, be achieved by peaceful means.

A few weeks after the founding of the MNC, in October 1958, Gaston Diori and Joseph Ngalula left for Accra to attend the All-African Peoples' Conference, summoned by Nkrumah shortly after the first Conference of Independent African States had taken place in Accra, in April 1958. Kwame Nkrumah who inspired the historic All-African Peoples' Conference has written about it as follows: 'From 5 to 13 December, I invited freedom movements and political parties in Africa to a conference in Accra. Delegates came from British, French, Belgian, Portuguese and Spanish colonial territories. This was the first All-African Peoples' Conference. What I had in mind was to give the forces of the liberation movement the strategy to move into action and the tactics for that strategy. ... It was to sound the clarion call for the advance and final assault on imperialism and the complete eradication of colonial oppression in Africa. Freedom fighters came from all over the continent and those who were then unknown are now the leaders, presidents and prime ministers of the colonized territory they represented. My object again was to infuse into the African Revolution new spirit and a new dynamism; and to create these where they were lacking.'[36]

At the Conference, Nkrumah made two significant points. Firstly he said: 'Ghana supports the struggle of the dependent peoples for the speedy elimination of imperialism, colonialism and the eradication from this continent of racialism. As I have always declared, even before Ghana attained her present sovereign status, the struggle for the independence of Ghana will be meaningless unless it is linked with the total liberation of Africa.' This then was the core of Pan Africanism. Secondly, in rejecting racialism, whether it be white or black he said: 'When I speak of Africa for Africans, it should be interpreted in the light of my emphatic declaration that I do not believe in racialism. The concept of Africa for the Africans does not mean that other races are excluded from it. It only means that Africans who are naturally in the majority in Africa shall and must govern themselves in their own countries.'

The Conference was attended among others by leaders of the national movements of Tanganyika, Zanzibar, Northern Rhodesia, Kenya, Angola, Spanish Guinea and Cape Verde Islands. All in all there were some 300 delegates representing the entire continent of Africa. Lumumba made a short speech where he denounced the balkanization of the Congo, and he ended his speech with the cry of: 'Down with colonialism, and imperialism; down with racism and tribalism; long live the Congolese nation; long live independent Africa.'

The Conference passed a number of resolutions, the most important being on imperialism and colonialism. But issues like tribalism and racialism were also considered. Thus on the question of tribalism, in order to combat the rulers' tactics of utilizing tribalism and religious separatism to perpetuate its colonial policy in Africa, a resolution called on political organizations, trade unions, cultural and other organizations, to educate the masses about the dangers of these evil practices. The independent governments were urged to pass laws, and through propaganda and education to discourage tribalism and religious separatism. Resolutions were also passed condemning traditional institutions which supported colonialism, and constituted organs of corruption, exploitation and repression.

On continental unity the Conference:

1. endorsed Pan-Africanism and the desire for unity among African people
2. declared that its ultimate objective was the evolution of a Commonwealth of Free African states;
3. called upon independent African states to lead the peoples of Africa towards the attainment of this objective;
4. expressed the hope that the day would dawn when the first loyalty of the African states would be to an African Commonwealth.

The main resolution condemned colonialism and imperialism in every shape and form, and stated that political oppression and economic exploitation of Africans by imperialist European powers should cease. It demanded universal adult suffrage be extended to all Africans, regardless of race and sex.

The most important paragraph of this resolution is as follows: 'The All-African Peoples' Conference in Accra declares its full support to all fighters of freedom in Africa, to all those who resort to peaceful means of non-violence and civil disobedience as well as those who are compelled to retaliate against violence to attain national independence and freedom for the people. Where such retaliation becomes necessary, the Conference condemns all legislation which considers those who fight for their independence as ordinary criminals.' The FLN of Algeria was represented at this Conference and it had embarked on the road of armed struggle. The resolution was a victory for its line of action.

The historic significance of this resolution should not be underestimated. The African leaders who were to become heads of states within a few years represented national movements whose method of struggle was passive resistance, and non-violence, like the authors of the Manifesto of the Congo. At that stage they looked for inspiration to Gandhi and Tolstoy rather than to Lenin, Mao Tse Tung or Ho Chi Minh. The FLN had embarked on the armed struggle against the French, but nevertheless the national movements from Kenya, Tanganyika, Nyasaland, Northern Rhodesia and Southern Rhodesia gave support to the Algerian method of struggle, even though their own was different. However this was not a specific instance with Algeria being an exception, but a general line to be followed. In other words, should the national movement take the road of armed struggle, then such a method of struggle should be given full support. By the time the Organization of African Unity (OAU) was formed in 1963, many more national liberation movements, notably Guinea Bissau and Angola had already embarked on this type of struggle. In fact, in the ensuing period, this form to liberate the remaining Africans under colonialism, became the only form of struggle which was given recognition in Africa, particularly in its southern part. The decks then were cleared at this historic Con•ference.

The Heads of Independent African States had already met in Accra in April of that same year and had passed a resolution on Algeria. It showed deep concern at the continuance of the war and the denial by France to the 'Algerian people of the right of independence and self determination despite various UN resolutions'. It called on France to enter into peaceful negotiations with the Algerian Liberation Front. While it recognized the right of the people to independence and self-determination, nevertheless it remained silent on the vital question of the use of armed force to achieve this very independence. The December resolution was thus a distinct advance, in that it committed future heads of state to recognize the legitimacy of this method of struggle.

81

The December 1958 All-African Peoples' Conference may be viewed as a continuation of the Pan-African Congress of 1945 held in Manchester, England. Kwame Nkrumah also played a leading part here as well. It was at this large gathering of intellectuals and workers' leaders from all parts of Africa and the Caribbean that the banner of independence and freedom was raised for all to see. In its Declaration to the Colonial Peoples of the World, drawn up by Nkrumah, it said:

'We believe in the rights of all peoples to govern themselves. We affirm the right of all colonial peoples to control their own destiny. All colonies must be free from foreign imperialist control, whether political or economic. The peoples of the colonies have the right to elect their own government, a government without restrictions from a foreign power. We say to the peoples of the colonies that they must strive for these ends by all means at their disposal ... the struggle for political power by colonial and subject peoples is the first step towards, and the necessary prerequisite to, complete social, economic and political emancipation.'

The All-African Peoples' Conference was an important landmark both ideologically and organizationally in the struggle for independence. The fact that Africans could meet on the soil of Africa to decide their own future in a country which was politicallly free, was itself an achievement. The delegates came from different parts of the continent, spoke different languages, had different traditions and religions, yet they probed and analysed problems from an All-African point of view. It is thus then that Pan-Africanism, as a part of the world wide anti-imperialist movement began to take shape. Organizationally, too, there was a distinct advance. The 300 delegates were not just intellectuals who represented only themselves, as was the case of the many who went to Manchester in 1945. In Accra, those who came represented national movements with mass followings. They were also the most conscious section of the national movement that the people were able to throw up. Thus after the Conference, they had to go and report to the people.

That is precisely what Lumumba did. He called a mass meeting immediately after his arrival in Leopoldville which was attended by some 7,000 people. There he gave his impression of the Conference, revealing clearly a qualitative leap that was taking place in his own outlook. He said: 'The Conference demands immediate independence for all Africa and that no country in Africa should remain under foreign domination after 1960. We state with satisfaction that the resolutions of the Conference coincide with the view of our movement. The independence that we claim in the name of peace cannot be considered any longer by Belgium as a gift, but on the contrary it is a right that the Congolese people have lost. The objective is to unite and organize the Congolese masses for the amelioration of their lot; the liquidation of the colonial régime and the exploitation of man by man. It is high time that the Congolese people prove to the world that they are cognisant of the realities of the autonomy gift which the government is preparing and promising.'

The Accra All-African Peoples' Conference thus cleared many a path, and brushed aside many an ideological cobweb. It clarified many important political issues as well as those involving political strategy. It however left a few important illusions. It did not bring up to date the latest development of imperialism in the era of the super US monopoly corporations, and the rise of the new and more dangerous predator, US imperialism. It therefore did not analyse the role of the United Nations from the point of view of who controlled it, and whose interests it served. Behind the verbiage of Charters and Freedoms, the question was who was manipulating it? How far was it different from the old and discredited League of Nations which revealed itself openly as a tool of imperialism? Chapter Eleven of the UN Charter made it clear that the interests of the inhabitants of the colonies were to be paramount and the direction should be to work towards self-government in accordance with the wishes of the majority of the inhabitants. The illusion was thus fostered that the UN stood for the independence and freedom of the colonial peoples. It was this illusion that was carried into the Congo by Lumumba, with tragic results for its people.

Lenin noted that apart from classical colonialism, where the export of capital was coupled with direct physical control of the territory, there was a second type, the semi-colony where the influence of finance capital was so decisive as to tie an outwardly independent country to the apron strings of the imperialist power.

The United States of America did not join with the other imperialist powers in the Scramble for Africa at the end of the nineteenth century. Nevertheless, it pursued a distinctly colonial policy, even though it had no colonies. In Latin America for instance, it made and unmade governments overnight through sheer weight of its financial resources, its financial aid and its links with the military hierarchy and oligarchies of the states. In other words, semi-colonies were established. After World War II, the US emerged as the colossus of the capitalist world. Its currency, the dollar, was as valuable as gold, and it was 'King'. Its economic growth, with the rise of the super monopoly corporations whose turn-over rivalled that of many medium states like Belgium itself, necessitated an expansion of spheres of influence and it could expand in the colonies of the former imperialist powers. Since the world was already parcelled out, there could be no division of the world, only re-division. The only way for the US to step in was for America to say that it stood for the abolition of the old type of colonialism. In so far as that was concerned, America did stand for independence. But it stood also for the other type of colonialism, political independence and economic control which is 'neo-colonialism'. The international agency to carry out this policy was to be the United Nations Organization.

The aspirations of certain layers of national liberation movements coincided with the broad strategy of American imperialism. And as long as this coincided, the UN played its part in decolonizing. But at times when they did not coincide and the interests of the colonial peoples clashed with not only the old imperialist powers but also with America, then the UN revealed the hidden claws of the American eagle.

That the US controlled the majority of the nations admitted to the UN need not be a serious matter for debate. Even now although defeated on the admission of China, its power is still very great. That it was able to keep out the Peoples' Republic of China for 22 years shows its strength and power. However, what is not generally known, is that it controls almost all the machinery to implement UN resolutions. Thus when the UN passes a resolution against the interests of American imperialism, then the administrative machinery of the UN is brought into play so as to render this resolution ineffectual and meaningless.

It is this illusion about the UN that was responsible for the letting into the Congo of the Trojan horse, in the form of UN troops which came on Lumumba's invitation. He found too late that with it came the CIA, and military personnel, who from an army of liberation turned out to be an army of occupation. Instead of restoring Lumumba to power by dislodging the régime of Moise Tshombe, it brought about the Congo Prime Minister's downfall, and his subsequent murder.

9

THE FORMATION OF THE MNC AND ITS PROGRAMME

LUMUMBA'S speech at Leopoldville in 1958, after he had returned from the Accra Conference, showed a new awakening and a new radicalization. Attempts to seal off the Congo from the winds of change were gone for good. The spirit of the Accra Conference had begun to infect increasing layers of the Congolese people. The MNC met in May 1959, and there one could see the impact of Accra. The programme, and the policy, show increasing clarity. More important, it also showed what society the MNC visualized for the Congo on the achievement of independence. It was only in October 1958 that the MNC was officially launched with Lumumba as its President. Early in that year he had left Stanleyville for the Congolese capital and soon established himself as a political figure. A Belgian with whom he had been associated remarked that he was insatiably interested in everything, and curious as an ethnographer. His fame as a writer, organizer and orator had preceded him. He joined the Federation des Batatela and was soon elected as its President. But unlike the other evolués, his aim in joining was to liquidate ethnic antagonism and to struggle for harmony among all, regardless of origin.

He also became a member of CEREA (Centre de Recherches Africaine) and there met Joseph Ileo and Joseph Ngalula, the leading figures of the Manifesto Group. Their views coincided with those of Lumumba at that time on many issues, particularly on the need to lead the Congolese towards consciousness of their national unity and responsibility. Before its actual formation, the MNC existed as an ideological tendency, with its members having little contact with the masses. Ileo and others were basically committee men who made no impact on the Congolese people at large. In Lumumba they found a man who was not only an established writer, but also a good organizer. However, he was elected by them because then he was 'the most eminent spokesman of liberal ideas.'

The MNC had broadened its scope. Its deputy President was Cyrille Adoula who was the Secretary-General of the trade unions. Besides Ileo and Ngalula, who were on the committee, there was also Alphonse Nguvulu. Others who associated themselves publicly were Gaston Diomi, President of Mutualités Chrétiennes, Antoine Ngwenza, Secretary-General des Employés Chrétiens, and Maximilian Lango, Vice-President of the Leopoldville section of APIC.

The MNC during its formation did not have a mass base like ABAKO, but it represented a step forward in the political consciousness of the people in that its leadership was drawn from the entire Congolese people, instead of a particular tribe, and therefore it could be rightly regarded as a truly national party. Secondly, it drew its support from the trade unions whose very basis of organization cut across tribalism.

The fundamental political aim of the MNC were:

(i) to liberate the Congolese people from the colonial régime, and to instal an independent democratic state:

(ii) to defend the fundamental liberties guaranteed by the Universal Declaration of the Rights of Man; individual liberty, freedom of association; formation of groups; and freedom of the press;

(iii) to struggle with all its power to guarantee the unity of the country;

(iv) to combat all manoeuvres towards balkanization, as well as all discrimination based on ethnic affiliation and race.

With regard to its economic aims, the MNC demanded:

(i) respect for the human individual without distinction of race, sex or religion, and condemned the exploitation of man by man;

(ii) the establishment of an economic régime based on the satisfaction of the needs of man, notably by equitable distribution of the Congolese national revenue;

(iii) the establishment of a single work code, and the equalization of salaries throughout the nation;

(iv) the utilization of the great riches of the country for the raising of the standard of living of the Congolese people;

(v) review and revision of all monopolies;

(vi) re-evaluation of agricultural products;

(vii) revision of the fiscal régime in order to redivide the public charges according to a progressive system. There were to be fiscal penalties for enterprises which maintained costly services outside the limits of the national frontiers;

(viii) the abolition of certain privileges held by firms;

(ix) respect for the reasonable rights of capital which is invested in the Congo, to the degree that it contributes to the raising of the standard of living of

the Congolese community. For the MNC recognized the right of capital to a reasonable profit.

In the social sphere, the MNC declared that there should
be a system of social security guaranteeing individual wel-
fare from the cradle to the grave; full employment; and
immediate assistance to the unemployed. The MNC condemned violently the passivity of the government which oppressed the poor classes with unemployment. All children
being equal, they must be allowed the benefit of equal protection and support. A new system of pensions and sickness
benefits was to be provided, more favourable to the older
worker. There was to be an amelioration of the rigorous
conditions for the granting of sickness benefits to those
whose incomes were insignificant; and a system of awards
for damages resulting from accidents while at work, and for
occupational illnesses, without discrimination of any sort.
The MNC considered the cost of health services to be a
public national responsibility. The receipt of medical care
should not depend on the income of the sick person. The
MNC went on to pledge itself to a programme to provide
the Congolese masses with decent, inexpensive housing. As
regards education, there was to be free, primary, secondary,
technical and advanced education; and compulsory school
attendance. Measures which limited schooling on the basis
of economic consideration, or of political opinion were to be
abolished. Parents were to be free to choose which kind of
education they wished for their children. Support was to be
given to youth organizations, and there was to be an 'in-
tensification of the education of the youth of the country.
The status of women was to be raised. Congolese arts,
customs, and traditional skills were to be promoted so long as
they did not restrict the liberty and advancement of the individual.

The difference in the Manifesto, and the new programme
of the MNC, lay in the fact that the former faced the Belgian rulers, and the latter the Congolese people. The Manifesto stated what would be acceptable to the liberal section
of the Belgian bourgeoisie; while the latter stated what

would be acceptable to the Congolese people. The programme of the MNC was all-embracing. It stood for the political liberation of the people, and also for the abolition of the exploitation of man by man. Its programme, therefore, covered political, economic and social aspects. What it had in common with the Manifesto was that it also stood for national unity. Where it differed radically and fundamentally was that it put the interests of the people before that of finance capital. In this vital distinction, imperialism saw the writing on the wall.

The MNC made no apologies about the fact that it considered the interests of the masses, the peasants and workers, to be decisive; and that it favoured the indigenous bourgeoisie as against foreign capital. In this policy may be seen a transitional programme which could be a step towards socialism.

In society there are two basic antagonistic forces, the rulers on the one hand, and the people on the other. In the Congo the rulers, the Belgian monopolists, were not only the exploiters but also the oppressors. But sandwiched between the two hostile forces stood the evolués, the rising Congolese bourgeoisie. Hitherto it had attached itself to the Belgian rulers. The publication of the programme of the MNC showed that a section of the evolués had detached itself from the rulers and had cast its lot with the people. And in doing so they had taken the logical step. They had formulated into programme and principles, the demands of the people in this particular stage of development.

For Lumumba this was a decisive and irrevocable break. Put up as the leading exponent of liberal ideas which in effect meant the ideas of the far-sighted from among the Belgian bourgeoisie, he now became their leading enemy. Although he made a short speech at the All-African Peoples' Conference in Accra, he impressed those whom he met in between official sessions of the Conference. Not only was he likeable as a person, but he was able to act as a bridge between the English and the French speaking delegates, for he spoke Swahili fluently. In the discussions he learnt the importance and absolute necessity to mobilize the masses who alone constituted a force to challenge the rulers. He realized that it was not enough for a liberation movement to say that it was a national movement, it had to be transformed into one by rallying all sections of the people into it. He also learnt something about tactics, and to distinguish between the principal foe and the lackey. One of his first acts after his return to the Congo after the Conference, was to make peace overtures to Kasavubu, the head of ABAKO.

To weld the people together it was necessary to unite all the possible organizations which were orientated towards the people and were political in character. In April 1959, he held a Congress of eight such organizations. These were Union Congolais; Parti Démocratique Congolais; Union Progressive Congolais, (UPECO); Union Economique Congolais (UNECO); and Mouvement National pour Protection des Milieux; and the MNC. It was here that a call was made for the installation of a Congolese government by January 1960 as a step towards complete independence. It was here that Lumumba said: 'It will be the responsibility of the government which the Congolese demand be installed by January 1960 to determine what date the Congo will accede to its independence.' This Conference called for adult suffrage, with a minimum age of 18, without distinction as to sex. The Conference also came out against tribal associations which were now beginning to transform themselves into political parties. A third motion declared its attitude towards the chiefs, and stated that traditional chiefs, unless elected, should be made members of the council only by a special statute.

The Conference represented a broad front of various sections of the population at different stages of development. Lumumba therefore did not have his way completely.

The MNC caught the imagination of the masses, and this could be seen in its organizational growth. The MNC of Ileo and Ngulula was confined to a small group of intellectuals based in Leopoldville. Now under Lumumba's dynamic leadership, which inspired all the youth that came into contact with it, branches were opened up in Kasai, Elizabethville, and one in Kolwezi. Orientale province was won over, and many of the future national leaders came from here. In Kivu province, MNC sections were set up in Bukavu, Pangi and Samba.

This was a period of going directly to the masses. Lumumba revealed his talents not only as a good organizer but also as a brilliant orator. Thus on 27th May, 1959, after returning from Brussels he stopped over at Coquilhatville, in the province of Equator, and won over the entire section of the Cercle des Amis du Progrès to the MNC.

In August he toured Kasai Province. Within a short period of a year the MNC was transformed into a national movement with a mass base. Its single asset undoubtedly was Lumumba, who with his enthusiasm, his ability to gauge the mood of the masses and respond to it, and his fiery oratory, led thousands of the uncommitted people to flock to the MNC. However the backbone of the party consisted of workers who entered the movement in a big way after 4 January 1959, when the populace of Leopoldville rose in revolt. These members of the MNC are nameless, but it is they who gave the MNC its drive and dedicated cadres.

The entry of the masses, and the transformation of the MNC into a people's party with a programme orientated towards the people brought about a split. As originally conceived, the MNC was to be a reformist national movement whose purpose it was to use the masses if necessary to put pressure on the Belgians to grant concessions to the evolués. The phenomenal growth of the MNC brought new elements into the party, who had no ties with the liberal bourgeoisie. They voiced the aspirations of the people, and Lumumba too was moving in this direction. But other founder members of the MNC had committed their thinking in such a way that they could not be anything but lackeys, and could not keep pace with the new thinking and mood. A break was inevitable. In any case the masters saw to it that the older leaders of the MNC cleared out. It had become too radical. A stage was reached when Joseph Ileo and those who shared his views had to choose the people, or their masters. They chose their masters and thus there occurred the first split in the MNC.

It was Lumumba, however, with the clarity of his demands who now brought things to a head. In June 1959, an attempt was made by eight organizations, including the MNC, to request the Belgian Government to grant individual liberties and universal suffrage. This was really a move to outflank the growing movement for total political independence. Lumumba sensed this accurately and therefore before a general assembly of the MNC he called for immediate independence, and denounced the saboteurs who were trying to delay this. On 13 July he elaborated this when he said: 'The Belgian Government in promising independence wishes to achieve it not through the aspirations and wishes of the Congolese people but according to their own aims. And what are these aims? To put in power white colonialists and black colonialists; to set up a puppet government in the framework of which the old colonial administration will continue to pull the strings, thanks to the marionettes which it will have placed in power. The régime will not be changed, only the actors.'

This was directed at Joseph Ileo, Moise Tshombe and others. The authors and the clique around the Manifesto group could not, and dare not, face the masses and claim that they did not stand for independence. They were essentially committee men and therefore through intrigues they sought to hamstring Lumumba so that they could still have the real power. They spread lies that Lumumba was dictatorial and was usurping the power of the central committee. They thus, under the guise of reorganizational measures 'In order to give equal weight to functional committees,' appointed their own men in certain posts. Lumumba saw this clever ruse and repudiated these manoeuvres. It was then that Ileo and his associates split off and came to be known as the 'Kalondji MNC.'

The split was a result of the growth of the MNC, and as such was beneficial to the organization. Rid of the elements of the liberal bourgeoisie who spent more time plotting than organizing, and who had become a break on the organization, the MNC was able to forge ahead. It could now rally the people for independence, and not for just a few concessions.

The Ileos could not tell the people the real reason why they split, that they did not want independence. Lumumba, it must be said, had no illusion about the Ileos. He knew that some day there would be a parting of the ways. He had thus launched his own journal the *Independence* based in Stanleyville. The result of the split, in fact really a breakaway, was that this clique found itself isolated once again from the people, and only found root in Kasai thanks to the financial support of the mining group which built up Kalondji as the Union Minière did Tshombe.

The authors and supporters of the Manifesto showed themselves up in their true colours. At the time when the interests of their masters demanded that there be a united Congo they stood up in support of national unity as recorded in the Manifesto. But when faced with a real national movement, they showed their true colours. They joined hands with the tribalists, for the rulers used tribalism to counter the nationalism of the people. Ileo and his companions joined hands with Kalondji who wanted a separate state in the Kasai.

At the close of 1959 a Congress of the MNC was held in Stanleyville. It was significant in that the MNC, having established a clear programme and policy, set about evolving methods of struggle. It was at this Conference, that the idea of a boycott of the elections to be held in December was accepted. The MNC had already become the pace-setter in calling for independence. This caught the imagination of the people, and all the parties had now to pay lip service to it. The idea of the boycott was already in the air. ABAKO and the PSA had already called for it. The Congress of the MNC also endorsed it. It read as follows: 'The Congress judges that as a result of a deliberate refusal of Belgium to accede to the political aspirations clearly expressed by the Congolese, Belgium has violated the Charter of the United Nations, notably article 73 para. B. The National Congress, supported by the popular masses which have decided to gain their immediate independence decided not to participate in the anti-democratic, anti-national elections, prepared by the Belgian Government with the sole aim of perpetuating the colonial régime in the Congo by artificial means . . . to vote in December is to vote against independence. Better to die than to continue to support the régime of subjection. The National Congress launches this day its plan for positive action for the immediate liberation of the Congo. It addresses a strong fraternal appeal to all the oppressed people of the Congo to mobilize themselves to put an end to Belgian domination.'

Lumumba's return to Stanleyville after a lapse of two years was a triumph, and it was here that the MNC made its greatest impact. As he drove to the city, observers noted that he drew wild demonstrations of support particularly from women for whom he had great personal appeal. It is understandable then that panic seized the Belgian authorities and the white settlers, particularly when after its Conference the MNC requested that permission be given to hold a mass meeting. When this was refused by the jittery authorities riots broke out, and the next day an armoured division, including nine tanks, was rushed to Stanleyville, the capital of the Orientale province. In the struggle, 26 Africans were shot dead and over 100 were hospitalized due to severe injuries from gunshot wounds. A warrant of arrest was issued to apprehend Lumumba for inciting this riot. There was no evidence whatsoever to support this charge, and the only crime was Lumumba's popularity with the people.

When it became known that the authorities were looking for him, Lumumba, unlike the passive resisters who voluntarily surrendered to arrest, just disappeared. If the authorities wanted him they had to get him. While he was underground, the people of Stanleyville became his forest, for they sheltered him. It is significant that the two people who played a very important part in saving him from arrest were Europeans. The MNC nationalism thus was cutting across colour lines, and was able to draw the best from the Europeans as well. These whites were subsequently arrested by the authorities and deported to Belgium.

The people made use of a traditional method of communication. Knowing that telephones were dangerous, they used the drum; the old method of communication under new conditions, and this was very effective. As his pursuers drew near, Lumumba was warned, and cleared off before his pursuers arrived.

But he was eventually arrested and sentenced to six months' imprisonment. While in detention he sent out instructions that the MNC should participate in the elections, and the result was that his party swept the boards winning 17 out of 18 seats in an almost 80 per cent poll. The PSA call for a boycott was outstandingly successful in Kivu. The MNC had now become, in a year, a power to be reckoned with in its own right.

A government can only rule effectively with the consent of the population. A stage was being reached in Stanleyville where the people were not prepared to give that consent. A writer describes this situation: 'From the time of the elections a cold war was being declared in Stanleyville between Africans, who were showing courage and audacity and the Europeans, who were finding themselves in a more and more difficult situation ... stones flew ... logs were left across roads and boards with nails sticking up were thrown in the streets ... purses were snatched as women walked down the streets in broad daylight ... the post office was systematically robbed of stamps. The MNC was setting up a file of undesirables in town ... undesirable Congolese were threatened with death after the Belgians had left.'

What had happened in Stanleyville was not an isolated incident. The Belgian authorities were being challenged all over the country as riots erupted in one place after another. The year 1959 was one of a revolutionary upsurge, which began with the mass struggle by the people of Leopoldville.

It dawned on the Belgians that under such a situation its paratroopers and tanks were of no avail. One incident could be cited to show their weakness and helplessness. King Baudouin of Belgium decided to visit the Congo a week before the December elections. His first stop was Stanleyville. There he was met with huge banners: 'Long Live Lumumba', who was in detention. The entire police and army had been brought out to protect the King, and therefore when riots again broke out the Congolese were in a position to take over the entire town of Leopoldville if they had only known how powerless the Belgians were at that moment. The far-sighted sections of the Belgian bourgeoisie drew proper conclusions from this incident. They saw two alternatives; either to accede to the demands for a political change, or to be prepared for an Algerian type of war. The lesson of the debacle that overtook the French at Dien Bìen Phu was not lost to them either. They thus opted for a constitutional change, and called for a Round Table Conference, hoping to salvage as much as possible by this method. What helped the Congolese national movement was that campaigns were also organized by the socialist and communist youth movements in Belgium that no soldier should be sent to the Congo. This agitation was also backed by the Socialist Trade Unions which were also opposed to the Congo going the way of Algeria.

The revolutionary upsurge in the Congo had weakened Belgium's hold in the Congo and now it was also faced with opposition within Belgium itself. It thus decided to retreat and agreed to a constitutional conference.

Four leading parties had been invited to the Round Table Conference. The ABAKO cartel which included the PSA and the PNP had eleven members each. The MNC by virtue of its massive electoral victory was now recognized, but it had only three; Tshombe's CONAKAT had two; CEREA and BALUBAKAT had one each. The rest consisted of minor parties and groups. At the time when the Conference opened, on 20 January 1960, Lumumba had begun to serve his six months' imprisonment. Eighty years of direct rule by the Belgians over the Congolese, a rule marked by barbarity and savagery that have few parallels in the world, was coming to an end.

The Brussels Round Table Conference

A feature of the Congolese national movement prior to independence, was the proliferation of political parties. At one stage, just before the elections in June 1960, there were over a hundred. At the time of the Brussels Round Table Conference there was no single party which had been able to rally the entire Congolese people. Parties like ABAKO and CONAKAT were tribal parties, and they made no attempts to organize nationally. It was from a position of weakness that the Belgians called the Conference, but the wily rulers believed that with such diversity, based on differences of language, religion and tribe, the parties would quarrel and bicker amongst themselves and therefore look to the rulers to be the judges and arbitrators. What they were losing in the Congo, through the 'crisis of confidence' they hoped to gain by this Conference. Furthermore, they had taken care to pack it with delegates from the moderate and conservative parties who could be relied upon to safeguard their interests. In this they made a big mistake. They had misjudged the growing political maturity that was taking place amongst the Congolese.

When the delegates arrived in Brussels they were surrounded by the Congolese students who were studying there. These were not only politically conscious, but also were in touch with world trends. More to the point, they pointed out the fundamental weakness of the Belgian rulers and that their tactic at the Conference was to prolong their rule by fomenting division amongst the parties. They therefore urged all the delegates to unite and to present a united Front. This went home, for the students acted not tribally but as spokesmen for the new Congolese nation. The result was that all the parties, including the PNP and CONAKAT, and the representatives of the chiefs, agreed to form a common Front. The minimum basis of the Front was that all should stand for immediate independence, and that whatever decisions should be reached would bind the Belgian Government. The Round Table Conference should not become a talking shop, and after the deliberations the resolutions should be implemented.

The result was that at this Conference the Congolese people, through their representatives, spoke with one voice before their rulers. It was the first time they had done so, and this magnificent unity shook the rulers and put them on the defensive. This unity was something rare amongst national movements negotiating for freedom.

While the Conference was in progress news reached the Conference that Lumumba had been sentenced to six months' imprisonment in Elizabethville, where his trial had taken place because Stanleyville was regarded as too dangerous. The MNC delegation asked that he be released forthwith. In this spirit of unity the entire Congolese delegation supported the move for his release. The Colonial Minister, Schryver, announced in an obvious effort to appease the delegates, that Lumumba could leave Elizabethville immediately. Two days later he was in Brussels to join the MNC and the other delegates, and amidst cheers told the conference that he fully supported the demand for independence. It was not long before Lumumba became the official leader and spokesman of the entire delegation.

At the Round Table Conference the Congolese leaders spoke bluntly and frankly. The language was tough and uncompromising. Kasavubu, leader of ABAKO said: 'Belgium must not think that she can always impose on the Congo what she wants. You think that you are giving us independence, but in fact independence is already being won.'

Ileo who had spent his entire political life serving his masters, and who was prepared to split away from the MNC rather than be reproached by his masters, threw caution to the winds and said that the Congolese were striking a hard bargain because they all remembered that the promises made had not been kept. For once he spoke like a man. And it was Paul Bolya, the leader of the right wing PNP who on behalf of the Front introduced the historic resolution, that independence to the Congo should be granted by 1 June 1960. Schryver on behalf of the Belgian Government agreed, with a small amendment that it should be on 30 June, a month later. This was accepted by the Front, and the final date for independence was fixed. Lumumba was happy for now they were coming back with independence in their pockets.

The basis of a common national movement is common oppression. It is this factor which unites all, irrespective of race, religion, tribe, culture, language and historical traditions. Such differences were accentuated by the rulers pursuing their policies of divide and rule. Differences such as these existed in the Congo. Nevertheless on this vital question of getting rid of the Belgians, their common oppressor, they were united. They acted as Congolese, and as Congolese they demanded independence from their common oppressor. It was because of this unity, that the Congolese achieved in one week, what could have taken a number of years.

In these very crucial days, not only were they able to secure the release of Lumumba, but they turned what was to be merely a consultative conference into a deliberative one. Instead of vague general promises, Belgium was now committed to a definite date for independence.

In Brussels then, in those crucial days of January 1960, the Congolese national movement, representing the various movements of workers, peasants and the bourgeoisie, pursued a single goal, and was able to achieve heights never scaled before. A solid Front of the Congolese people had forced the Belgians to give way. When Bolya called for independence, he for once was not voicing the demand of his own small class but also the demand of the Congolese worker and peasant; in fact the demand of the entire Congolese nation.

But the rulers had learnt their lesson. They had taken too much for granted. They understood that from the pressure of the people, even hardened collaborators could wilt and turn against them. But they had a six full months ahead of them. During this time they redoubled their efforts, and the entire Belgian ruling class, from the monopolists to the administrators and settlers, moved *en masse* to smash this unity of the Congolese people.

10

THE STRUGGLE FOR THE MASSES

ANOTHER reason why the Belgian rulers agreed to the demand for independence was because they believed that the parties they were sponsoring would carry the elections, and that these would be able to look after their interests. They were convinced that the PNP (Parti National Progrès) which had welded all the right wing groupings together, and tribal parties like CONAKAT, would be able to form the first government. The PNP and other right wing groups had also this same belief, and that is one reason why it was Bolya who sponsored the independence resolution.

Classes create their own institutions in political, educational and social spheres to carry out their policies. Parliament as an institution arose to suit the needs of the bourgeoisie in its struggle against feudalism. After the bourgeoisie captured power it retained this institution to legalize its policies and measures. The granting of the franchise to the workers and poor peasants after a bitter struggle, however, did not alter its essential role. Rather it gave the bourgeoisie in one sense a longer lease of life, for it fostered the illusion amongst the workers, that this institution was theirs, and that the government was also theirs.

The bourgeoisie has vast financial resources as well as numerous links with various institutions in society. For instance, they have the free use of halls, as well as the services of the press. Through these, as well as by the corruption of leaders of the working class, they have been able to see that the right government comes to power.

In the Congo, besides the State machinery which would be helping the puppet parties, there was the intervention of Big Business, in the form of the big monopolies. It became vital to them that the right party was swept in, which would not be a danger to their economic interests. So high were the stakes that the Union Minière made only the slightest attempt to conceal the fact that it poured millions into the coffers of the right wing parties. It was not by accident that Kasavubu went to see Tshombe during this period. The mining bosses wanted to have a good look at him, this 'King of the Congo', before giving him any money. The Annual Report of Union Minière for 1960 says: 'that exceptional expenditures were incurred through the political events in the Congo in July 1960, composed mainly of expenses of evacuating members of our personnel and their families, expenses for their return and various allowances – amounting to 2.5 million dollars.'

The real facts of this evacuation were that the company personnel were evacuated by road to a place about 200 miles away, and were back at their jobs after a few days. It is clear then that this vast sum of money could not have been spent on evacuation. It was not only CONAKAT that received money, although it could have been the largest beneficiary, but other right wing parties also received some. And what applied to Union Minière could also apply to the other monopolies operating in the Congo. Kalondji's splinter group, for example, received money from Forminière in the Kasai.

The Belgian settlers also gave liberally. Suddenly for a certain strata of the Congolese – the careerists – politics began to have its lucrative side. Some of them openly touted for financial support. Thus B. Makonya approached a spokesman of the white settlers with: 'Il faut que ces Messiers nous donnent de l'argent, cinq million francs ou plus, pour activer propagande a l'interior, car les interêts que nous dependons sont les interêts du Katanga, sans distinction de race, ou de couleur.'[37] With such massive financial backing from the monopolists as well as the white settlers, and State interference in many other ways, Belgium was confident that the elections would produce favourable results.

Here again, the rulers made another cardinal mistake. They had confused their private wishes for reality. They had underestimated the wind of change that was sweeping the country. They underestimated the impact the MNC was making on the Congolese population with its programme of independence, drastic social and economic reforms, and the call to end authoritarianism. The Belgians still believed that with the split in the MNC, the organization had lost its best leaders, thinkers and organizers. But one writer pointed out: 'The several Congresses held by the MNC in the months of April and May 1960 were intended not only to provide its leader with a forum for the ventilation of his grievances, they were also intended to bring the masses into contact with Lumumba's personality, which alone constituted the MNC's most valuable asset during the campaign. His ability to sense and articulate the demands of his public, coupled with his talent for meeting a wide range of expectations was a key element in the popular appeal of the MNC. Above all, Lumumba possessed a special knack for setting people in motion, for arousing an emotional response from his audience, for whipping up enthusiasm for his ideals. His own excitement as well as his own ideas was infectious.'[38] In other words it was Lumumba's own dynamic behaviour which helped to score a victory at the polls.

If Lumumba inspired the people it is because he himself was inspired by the cause that was before him, that of the upliftment of a people under slavery for decades, through the removal of oppression and exploitation. He had come to recognize the people as the only force that would be able to challenge the ruling class. Therefore he went all out to mobilize them and to instil in them the confidence that with their unity it was possible to achieve their aspirations. The people too, were also in the process of awakening. Ideologically the Congo was in a state of ferment, and the people were in the frame of mind to grasp at the boldest and most advanced ideas, and to make them their own. If in Lumumba they found the man they were looking for, it was because Lumumba, more than any other Congolese leader, had his fingers on the pulse of Africa, and through it could also feel the Congo's own heart beat. He listened to the people, and understood their local problems. But he placed these against the wider background of the national problem, showing that this could be solved if they pooled their efforts at the national level.

If Lumumba was a talented organizer and a powerful speaker, he was equally an excellent pupil. He had been inspired by Kwame Nkrumah and Sékou Touré, and other Pan-Africanists, and was quick to assimilate the latest experiences and ideas from these quarters. He learnt that it was permissible within the framework of one's policy to make certain tactical shifts and alliances with one's political opponents. Thus he forged alliances with smaller parties and groupings like Union Congolais Kasai, Mouvement Politique Koinoka, Alliance de Basque and Coalition Kasameni.

In the process of alliances he showed great flexibility on a number of issues. Thus, while the MNC stood for a centralized state, it now stated that it stood for a certain degree of regioal autonomy for all the six provinces. In this way it cut away the plank of a number of tribal parties.

It was however on the issue of the chiefs that Lumumba showed great tactical skill. He recognized that they were a force to be reckoned with, even though the rapid march of history was slowly pushing them aside. The programme of MNC had indicated the general stand. But at the Luluabourg Congress held between 3–4 April 1960, the MNC made a tactical shift. This may be seen in the resolution which stated that Congress recognized that the participation of customary authorities in political institutions was necessary to ensure social equilibrium and stability. The resolution, however, warned the chiefs not to fall a prey to corruption or to become victims of colonial propaganda.

The tenor of this was clear. The rulers believed that all radicals, because of their inexperience, would fall on the question of the chiefs, because no progressive would have any truck with them. But Lumumba separated his principal enemies from his opponents, from the conscious, to the politically ignorant. As a result of the resolution, Lumumba showed himself to be against Belgian rule but not against customary leaders. This cut the PNP to pieces, for it was pro-Belgian as well as pro-chiefs.

Lumumba in this period was able to bring to bear two powerful forces which played an important part in the elections and which were to form the backbone of his leadership. First, he mobilized and regrouped the youth into a vast nationwide youth movement. The Jeunesse Mouvement National Congolais was formed to provide the youth with ideas of citizenship and patriotism. Secondly, he established the Union Nationale des Travailleurs Congolais, and this linked up with the World Federation of Trade Unions, and

UGTAN based in Conakry. The entry of the youth and the workers, with their own organizations, had the effect of seeing that the MNC kept veering towards the people organizationally and ideologically.

Apart from the one at Luluabourg, Congresses were held at Coquilhatville, Ininongo and Stanleyville, to mobilize support for the forthcoming elections. It was emerging as a party which stood to eliminate Belgian rule but which was not against individual Belgians. It was against the Belgians as oppressors, but wanted those Belgians who were prepared to help the country to stay. In this way, it was able to attract the most nationally-conscious section of the population into its fold. The socialists too would find little fault with this. On the other hand it extended its hand of friendship to the conservative layers of the population, the chiefs, who hitherto were used as instruments by the Belgians. They too knew that the Belgians were to depart and therefore could not actively oppose the MNC. In short, many of them were neutralized. What in 1958 was an idea in the minds of a few conscious intellectuals, eighteen months later was rapidly becoming a reality. A national movement, uniting workers and peasants, intellectuals, youth, women, chiefs and civil servants, was surfacing under the aegis of the MNC. And it was this Front that went to the polls in 1960, the most crucial year in the history of the Congolese people.

11

TRIBAL NATIONALISM

IN the main, the parties that Lumumba had to face were tribal parties. Not having acquired sophistication, some of these did not try to hide their tribal politics behind grand sounding names like 'National'; 'Democratic'; or 'Progressive'. The ABAKO was thus the Alliance des Bas-Kongo; CONAKAT, the Confédération des Associations Tribales du Katanga, and BALUBAKAT, the Association des Baluba de Katanga. The breakaway wing, which stole the name of the MNC, carrying the name of Kalondji, also degenerated into a tribal party.

Hitherto, socialists have passed off the phenomenon of tribalism believing that it was a dying force which, like other anachronistic institutions would be swept away. But with independence, far from dying, it has grown in proportions and intensity, becoming at times the central problem facing Africans on the road of national reconstruction. It has become evident that it cannot be ignored any more.

Nkrumah in his *Class Struggle in Africa* has given the problem the attention it deserves. He has made a valuable contribution in drawing a clear distinction between tribes and tribalism. Of the former he says 'There were tribes in Africa before imperialist penetration ... Tribes, like nationalities may always remain in a country, but it is tribalism – tribal politics – that should be fought and destroyed. Under a socialist Union Government of Africa, tribalism, not tribes, will disappear.'[38] Tribalism was a different matter for it arose 'from colonialism, which exploited feudal and tribal survivals to combat the growth of national liberation movements ... workers were kept in tribal or traditional structures, and in reservations, in an attempt to prevent the growth of class consciousness.'[40] Nkrumah adds: 'At Independence, the colonial powers again fostered separatism and tribal differences through the encouragement of federal constitutions.'[41] In this post Independence period he says, however: 'In the era of neo-colonialism, tribalism is exploited by the bourgeois ruling classes as an instrument of power politics, and as a useful outlet for the discontent of the masses. Many of the so-called tribal conflicts in modern Africa are in reality class forces brought into conflict by the transition from colonialism to neo-colonialism. Tribalism is the result, not the cause, of underdevelopment.'[42] Nkrumah could well have been speaking with the Congo in mind.

Capitalism in its struggle against feudalism, claimed that it stood for a higher form of society by annexing science and technology and using these as weapons to overthrow the nobility. But once in power, it showed extraordinary interest in 'primitive and savage societies'. It is these very societies which were the objects of conquest in the 'Scramble for Africa'. In this modern atomic and jet age, study of such societies of the past is being given an honourable and dignified place in the universities. Anthropology is being pushed aside, and young intellectuals are being given liberal grants, and every other facility, to do research on the various tribes in Africa. Volumes have appeared on the customs, languages, traditions and various other social customs. Particular attention is being paid to the tribal record of resistance to colonization, Christianity, and inter-tribal relationships.

It has become clear that this research has been far from disinterested, whatever may have been the motives of the researchers themselves. The colonial powers have used this vast data at their disposal to implement the policy of divide and rule, pitting one tribe against another, chieftainship against the working class and the intellectuals, and then the intellectuals against the workers and peasants.

Capitalism produced the proletariat, imperialism has produced the modern national movement. Both these were inevitable, for both are part of a historical process which cannot be reversed. The rulers from experience know that they cannot stop the flow of the stream of history. They have decided, therefore, to channel it, so that it does not pose a threat to them. They too have intervened on the canvas of history, but only to be able to delay the inevitable. Thus on the one hand, they prevented the workers from forming trade unions where they would be able to present a common Front against the employers, and on the other hand they have pitted workers against their fellow workers, using tribalism as the instrument of division. Against the national liberation movement, they stimulated tribal nationalism.

It would not be correct to state that tribal nationalism reflects the political consciousness of people in a particular stage of development. Most of these tribal parties were formed in the late fifties in the Congo. Yet the Congolese had religious movements with a political programme as early as 1923, as in the case of the Kitawala movement, which cut across all tribal barriers. This started off in Katanga and spread to all the major towns in the Congo. By 1936, reports said that the compounds of the workers living in Union Minière in Jadotville were infected with Kitawalist cells. They were preaching equality of salaries, and Africa for the Africans. Emile Lunga, one of its leaders, harassed and imprisoned said: 'We blacks are here in our country and what we want is to be considered as Europeans, for the Bible makes no distinction between white and black. Our Watch Tower movement seeks to put an end to all this. For it is here only in the Congo that the government considers the natives as slaves.' Here Lunga was asking for an end to discrimination when he called for equality between white and black.

The Kitawala movement was involved in a major insurrection in Orientale and Kivu Provinces in 1944. Its national character could be seen by the action that the Congolese Government took against the movement. By provincial edicts it banned the movement in Katanga in 1937; in Orientale in 1943; in Kivu in 1944; in Equator 1946; and in Leopoldville in 1948. The Kitawala, like the fifty other movements which suffered persecution mercilessly at the hands of the rulers, was essentially a religious movement making political demands. Their failure lay in that they looked to the past instead of the future. But as in the case of the Kitawala movement it was the workers and peasants who took it up and used it as their instrument. However, even with their limitations, it does show that a genuine movement springing from the soil can, and does, cut across tribal and other barriers. The Kitawala had adherents from all the tribes of the Congo.

By the late fifties, the rulers could not hold back the growth of political parties. They thus created tribal organizations and turned them into political parties. In this way they hoped to get a section of the bourgeoisie to defend their interests. In early 1958, Moise Tshombe formed CON-AKAT. One of the reasons for this was that the elections held in 1957 in Elizabethville were won by individuals from the Kasai province. The slogan of his party was: 'Katanga for the Katangans'. Tshombe came from a wealthy family. His father owned a chain of retail stores, a fleet of buses, hotels, and plantations. Tshombe himself was trained as an accountant and went into business. But he became insolvent very soon. He was also linked up with chieftainship through marriage. His wife was the daughter of Chief Mwata Yawa Nawezi III, described as the most prestigious of the Congo chiefs. In 1966 he made a two-month trip to the US under the sponsorship of a Protestant mission. He was a major supporter of CONAKAT. Tshombe thus represented the most reactionary forces in Congolese society, and it is small wonder that Union Minière gave him and his party full support.

At times Tshombe gave the impression that he stood for the independence of the Congo, but he advocated the total decentralization of powers in order to prepare future federated states before the proclamation of independence. In other words, he wanted independence only after the interests of the Union Minière had been secured.

CONAKAT was a federation of tribes. But it did not last, and in 1959 the BALUBAKAT split from CONAKAT— leaving it with the Lundas. An observer commented on Tshombe's Party as follows: 'Conakat ... demands the creation of a federal state within the framework of which the province of Katanga would be directed and administered by authentic Katangan citizens, to the exclusion of all members of other races or tribes, and would have the right to separate itself from the rest of the Congo if the defence of Katangan interests made it necessary.' In other words, if the interests of the Union Minière demanded it, then Katanga would secede, for the interests of Tshombe and the Company had become synonymous.

At the Round Table Conference in Brussels, CONAKAT went about making public the telegrams it received from some of its supporters. One such read: 'The Round Table is useless. The people of Katanga judge that the only solution is the independence of the Congo. Let us form immediately a Katangan government.' Thirty-two whites sent a similar appeal: 'If there is stalemate at the Round Table, we stand behind you for a future independent Katanga.'[43]

Even before independence, therefore, Tshombe hoisted the flag of secession. For pressure was being exerted even at the time of the Round Table Conference for the secession of Katanga. It was not the interests of the people which demanded this, but that of the mining monopolies and the reactionary bourgeoisie of Katanga.

Tshombe revealed his racialism when he wanted the exclusion of all races and tribes from the government of Katanga. But it was racialism and tribalism directed against his fellow Congolese, and not against the whites. The independent Congo he visualized would be within the framework of the Belgo–Katangese community. In fact it would be the alliance of the Lunda bourgeoisie with the Belgians, against the entire Congolese people. Moise Tshombe and the bourgeoisie of Katanga revealed their ties, as well as their role. Their class interests tied them to imperialism, and their role was to whip up tribalism, to separate the Lunda people from the rest of the Congolese. In this way the tribalism of CONAKAT struck at the national movement of the Congolese. While this was the case, it saw to it that it remained under the white Belgians. In short, CONAKAT adopted the racialism of the rulers, their tactics of divide and rule, and used it against the Congolese, but not against the whites, their inspirers.

The tribalism of CONAKAT was clear, and so was its association with the colonizers, the chiefs and the big monopolists. This discredited it in the eyes of the masses of the Congo. At one stage, even right wing politicians did not want to show their open associations with Tshombe. However, it was not so with ABAKO led by Kasavubu. While tribal in outlook ABAKO played an important part in the awakening of the Congolese masses, even though its activities were confined to the Ba-Kongo tribe. Up to December 1959 the Belgians feared it more than any other political party. President Nkrumah invited the leaders to the Accra Conference of 1958, and while the Belgian authorities allowed Lumumba and his associates to fly to Accra, Kasavubu was prevented because 'his papers were not in order'.

The strength of ABAKO lay in the fact that a large section of the Ba-Kongo were urbanized. Leopoldville for instance, had 50 per cent of the population from this tribe. It is estimated that prior to independence about one and a quarter million Ba Kongo lived around Leopoldville and the Lower Congo.

Far sighted sections of the rulers, afraid of the growth of a proletariat with a national and a class consciousness, encouraged the growth of an organization which was purely tribal in character. ABAKO was founded in 1950. It stood for the rebirth and unification of the Ba-Kongo language. Literacy here was amongst the highest in the Congo; 54 per cent in Leopoldville, and 37 per cent in the other areas. They thus were able to publish newspapers like *Congo Diu; Notre Congo* and *Congo Diet.*

ABAKO, in standing for the rebirth and unification of the language of the Ba-Kongo showed that it hankered for the past glories of a once powerful empire. It believed that the Kongo Kingdom of the fifteenth and sixteenth centuries could be revived. Nlandu, the founder of ABAKO— said that the Ba-Kongo would again be a 'great and prosperous nation in Africa.'

If this attracted a certain strata of intellectuals it also made the masses gravitate there. Political parties were in general banned, and the people, therefore, joined what they could. But their entry gave ABAKO a political orientation. This also coincided with Kasavubu taking over the leadership in 1954. He had been known to the masses as the radical who had spoken about the right of the first occupant as early as 1946.

ABAKO came out against the Manifesto of the MNC with its counter Manifesto, and said harshly and sharply: 'For us, we don't wish to collaborate in the elaboration of the plan, but simply to annul it because its application would serve to retard the Congo. It is the same old lullaby ... emancipation should be granted us this very day, rather than delayed another thirty years.'

It further scoffed at the Manifesto's aims in trying to achieve emancipation through constitutional and non-violent means, and it characterized its supporters as 'soldiers who love victory, but who renounce arms'. In 1957, organizing tribally, ABAKO swept the polls in parts of Leopoldville, resulting in Kasavubu becoming the Mayor of Dendale. It was ABAKO which refused to cooperate with the Belgians. Kasavubu said again and again: 'I demand independence and the departure of all Belgians.' In the 1959 elections, ABAKO and the PSA boycotted the elections.

The prestige and popularity of ABAKO shot up after the January 1959 upsurge. It was Lumumba's speech which fired the peoples imagination, but it was ABAKO which reaped the credit largely through the wave of repression which the authorities launched. ABAKO was banned, some of its leaders were imprisoned, others were banished. Kasavubu was sent to Belgium. Here the rulers had a close look at him to find out whether he had a price. ABAKO in the main went underground, and many fled across the river to the neighbouring Congo Brazzaville which had a large Ba-Kongo population. It was here that Youlou, then President of Congo Brazzaville, and described as more French than the French, built an alliance and later infiltrated ABAKO. Meanwhile, Kasavubu was being built up in the USA, and one correspondent described him as the 'King' of the Congo.

ABAKO was nationalistic in that it wanted an end of Belgian rule, and spearheaded a move towards independence. But its tribal policies put it in a position where it was in opposition to the independence of the entire Congo, and wanted it to be applied to the Ba-Kongo only. It did not want to wait for the other areas to join in. It wanted to go it alone. Thus the tribalism of Tshombe and the tribalism of Kasavubu met at a certain point, for both wanted a dismemberment of the Congo. And when the centralized state did take place, it was ironical that both these tribalists became President and Prime Minister of the Congo at a certain stage.

The arrest of Kasavubu and other leaders led to an increased radicalization of ABAKO. There was an element which emerged that said that it would use any means to bring about the realization of its aims. Reports reached Brussels that it was on the point of launching a civil disobedience movement. It demanded that its separate state be recognized as independent as from January 1960. That this threat was there, was recognized by the government itself.

On the other hand, the far sighted section of the Belgian rulers, as well as the monopolists, realized that they had soon to come to terms with the ABAKO leadership. The Governor-General, Schoeller, wrote about his visit to the lower Congo: 'One single thing counted, immediate independence; one single person was competent to decide everything, Mr Kasavubu .. his personality is now veritably deified, the object of blind and fanatic mass submission.'

The Ba-Kongo were not only the most urbanized but also the most detribalized section of the Congolese people. Even in the rural areas, chieftainship as an institution had almost disappeared. Yet Kasavubu thought it fit to revive tribalism with its ceremonial rituals. Photographs of Kasavubu were widely circulated. A typical one showed Kasavubu seated on a throne placed on a leopard skin on a carpeted dais, receiving oral petitioners on their knees. 'One hears rumours in Leopoldville that he is related to a clan from whence chieftainship is drawn; this tale is interesting for its existence not its veracity.' There were also pictures circulating showing Saint Peter giving the Keys of the Kingdom to Kasavubu.

The Belgians however, summed him up correctly when one of them said that Kasavubu, although a nationalist, was not by nature a revolutionary and did not have a dynamic temperament. In other words, they saw that Kasavubu could be bribed and corrupted, and relied upon to maintain capitalism in the Congo. Scratch a tribalist and you find an aspirant capitalist.

The Belgians sent him back to the Congo. But it was a different Kasavubu, and not the picture that the people had of him as one who was bold, fearless and uncompromising. At the Congress of ABAKO held in December 1959, Kasavubu, now softened and mellowed said: 'It is to the Belgian people that we address ourselves and of whom we think at this moment. They are a courageous and a proud people

1 *President Kwame Nkrumah and Patrice Lumumba, Prime Minister
of the Congo, in Accra in August 1960, when they signed a secret
Agreement to form a Union of Ghana and the Congo*

2   *Patrice Lumumba, leader of the MNC, speaking to Party members at Okbar on 18th June 1960*

3 Patrice Lumumba is greeted by his children at his home in Leopoldville on 8th August 1960, after returning from his visits to the USA and Independent African countries

4 *Pauline Lumumba being led away weeping after a memorial to Patrice Lumumba had been dedicated by Antoine Gizenga in Stanleyville, 9th May 1961*

who have never recoiled before great sacrifices in order that their rights and liberties could triumph.'

Such speeches came from the Congolese lackeys before 1958. The people, particularly in the Lower Congo, had passed through this stage and had had a taste of extreme and brutal Belgian terror, which they had replied to by intensifying underground work to carry out political agitation. Kasavubu's sentiment was thus completely out of step with the mood of the Congress. The entry of an entirely new generation of youth, radicalized and even nationalistic, made itself felt at this Congress. The resolutions passed were far reaching and called for the total independence of the Congo, and the formation of a provisional government based on federal principles. Europeans were to be debarred from voting. Another radical stand was on the economy. Its preamble said that the Congo was a capitalist state, and that the economy of the Congo should be orientated towards the satisfaction of the needs of man, and not towards individual profit.

If the Conference then did not reject Kasavubu the Man, it certainly rejected his overtures of collaboration with the Belgian rulers. A left wing was developing in ABAKO which had much in common with the politics of the MNC. The same could also be said of the PSA. Some of its members were to become Lumumba's pillars of strength in his struggle against the forces of counter-revolution.

Both Kasavubu and Tshombe had this in common, they were both educated, the former as an accountant, the latter in a Catholic seminary. They were therefore in a position to know that tribalism had no place in modern society. But their rank opportunism was such that they did not scruple to use this for their own ends to advance the cause of their own respective bourgeoisie, at the expense of the interests of the Congolese workers and peasants. By their appeal to the tribe, they retarded the growth of a national Congolese consciousness. Kasavubu when it suited him stood for modernism, thus endearing himself to the rising generation of honest intellectuals. On the other hand, before illiterates, he behaved like an oriental monarch, despotic and demanding complete obedience.

The end of the decade of the fifties showed Belgian imperialism in a state of crisis. Hence it threw all caution to the
winds and stood its puppets right in the front line. Tshombe
said he stood for Katanga for the Katangans, while Kasavubu dreamt of the revival of the Kongo Kingdom. Outwardly, there was nothing that bound Tshombe and
Kasavubu together, but immediately after the Round Table
Conference, Kasavubu paid a visit to Katanga at a time
when the party leaders were up to the neck organizing for
the elections. But the A B A K O leader was coming to his
masters, the Union Minière, who wanted to size him up.
They wanted a Kasavubu-Tshombe team to head the future
governments of the Congo, an alliance which would perpetuate the system of exploitation in the country.

The very force that kept the Lunda and Ba-Kongo
people from coming together, and from joining with the rest
of the Congolese, now brought their leaders together. Faced
with a mass upsurge of the workers and peasants, whose
pressure was being shown in the radical resolutions on political and economic matters not only in the M N C – but also in
A B A K O, it became imperative that a Front of moderate
Parties be formed to counter this 'extremism'.

A 'moderate' and 'extremist' in this Congolese context
meant the class position each group took in relation to the
workers and peasants on the one hand, and the Belgian
rulers and their monopolies on the other hand. The radical
parties, and sections within parties, were moving to a position where independence was not enough. It should be an
instrument in the elimination of the exploitation of man by
man. In the face of this onslaught, the Tshombes, the Kalondjis, the Kasavubus already divested of their tribal cloaks,
united to strike, even at their own fellow tribesmen, who
with their radicalism threatened the interests of their
masters. As the nationalist phase of the struggle was drawing
to a close with the preparations for elections granting independence, class divisions surfaced, and it was this split in the
Congolese parties which brought about a new realignment
of forces.

The tribalists abandoned secession, attended the Round

Table Conference and also participated in the elections. They all called for an independent Congo with federal power to the provinces. They did so because they believed that they would head the new Congo Government, and federalism would guarantee a division of spoils for the bourgeoisie of the various tribal groupings. Thus the Ba-Kongo bourgeoisie would have the whole of the Lower Congo as a field of exploitation, and competition from the others would be prevented.

The tribalists believed in their victory because that is what their masters had promised them. They too had an inflated opinion of their strength. They were also confident that with the massive funds put at their disposal by the monopolists, they would be able to sweep the polls. Instead of being heads of Little Katangas and Little Kongo Kingdoms they began to groom themselves for the roles of presidents and prime ministers of a united Congo.

But the elections in May 1960 showed that the Belgians made disastrous miscalculations, paralleled only by the French in Guinea. Here too, in the Congo, the rulers underestimated the political consciousness of the Congolese people, and were beaten in a game where they appeared to have all the trumps.

12

TRIUMPH OF THE MNC

THE results of the May 1960 elections for the Congolese National Assembly, showed the following: see page 116.

The Belgians, were reluctant to publish the number of votes each party received although they had the information. They kept it to themselves, releasing it only three years later. This is understandable, for the composition of the National Assembly did not correctly reflect the landslide victory for the MNC, and the crushing defeat of the tribal and puppet parties. The figures released by Ganshof, the

Minister of Belgium in charge of Congolese affairs show the following:

Party	Leopold-ville	Equa-tor	Orient-ale	Kivu	Kat-anga	Kasai	Total
MNC	1	2	21	5	—	4	33
PSA	13	—	—	—	—	—	13
ABAKO	12	—	—	—	—	—	12
CEREA	—	—	—	10	—	—	10
PNP	—	2	3	—	—	3	8
CONAKAT	—	—	—	—	7	—	7
KALONDJI	—	—	—	—	—	8	8
BALUBAKAT	—	—	—	—	6	—	6
Miscellaneous	7	14	1	8	3	7	40
Total	33	18	25	23	16	22	137

	votes		votes
MNC	521,381	CONAKAT	104,870
PSA	278,971	CEREA	95,729
ABAKO	210,542	PUNA	92,547
PNP	178,237	BALUBAKAT	80,434
KALONDJI	147,578		

From this it can be seen that the MNC polled more votes than the openly tribalistic parties like ABAKO, CONAKAT and the KALONDJI party. It was these, together with the rightist PNP, which received thousands of dollars from the monopolists operating in the Congo. Lumumba's MNC stood for an avowedly anti-tribalist programme of national unity. The people thus were presented with two clear alternatives, and between a national and a tribal party, chose the former. In this then, one sees the political maturity of the Congolese masses. Secondly, in the urban areas around Leopoldville, the people returned the PSA, for although at one stage it was allied to the ABAKO cartel, it now stood for a radical economic programme to eliminate the exploitation of man by man. In this sense then the people also voted for national democratic programmes and policies.

The result also indicates that the split in the MNC which ideologists of the bourgeoisie still present as a weakening of the MNC, rather than harming the organization had in fact strengthened it, for it went to the people united with one voice, which in fact was their voice. On the other hand, the tribal parties found themselves split. There was a split in ABAKO after the Round Table Conference when the youth revolted against the authoritarianism of Kasavubu. CONAKAT too could not speak for the Katangese as a whole, for BALUBAKAT seized 40 per cent of the vote in that province. It was this division in ABAKO which gave the MNC a foothold right in Leopoldville province.

Bourgeois democracy with its institution, the parliament, is in fact a dictatorship of the minority over the majority. But it exercises this dictatorship through the 'consent of the majority'. This is achieved through parliamentary elections usually once in every five years. The bourgeoisie, though a minority, controls the means of production and as a result has vast resources at its disposal. It allows opposition parties to operate, within a distinct framework, that they will not touch or harm the sacred right of property.

But behind all this parliamentarianism stand the armed forces and the police, instruments of coercion and suppression. These are brought into play when the people, because of their political awareness and consciousness, see through the façade and elect those who really represent them. More so when they score such massive victories as to elect them to become the government of the country. Then the bourgeoisie shows its teeth and claws. The armed forces are brought into play to overthrow the popularly elected governments. It happened in Spain in 1936, when Fascist Franco overthrew the legally elected government. It was the first. It was not going to be the last.

The Belgian bourgeoisie in Brussels and the Congo had bungled the elections in completely underestimating the political consciousness of the Congolese people. They were so busy 'moderating' Kasavubu with thousands of pounds, building up Tshombe, and weaning away Kalondji, that they forgot the MNC. They believed that with the defection of Ileo and his coterie of incorrigible agents of the liberal bourgeoisie, the MNC had lost its leadership for good. Now with the election results out, Belgium looked foolish in the eyes of Britain, France and other colonial powers. These had taken care to see that the leaders whom they had groomed to take over power would be relied upon to continue the relationship with the mother country, that is to protect their economic interests. Belgium was attacked precisely because of its shortsightedness and unparalleled greed in not building up rapidly enough a middle class, and grooming a political leadership to take over. The fact is, Lumumba won despite rigging, bribery and corruption, and despite a campaign of 'slander' that the MNC was communist. The electoral victory meant a triumph of nationalism but also of Pan-Africanism.

The imperialists realized quickly what this victory meant. If the Congo under Lumumba was to be given a breathing space to consolidate itself, then not only the Congo but the entire continent of Africa could be jeopardized for capitalism and imperialism. The Congo had minerals, some of which like uranium, were of a strategic nature. Imperialism as a whole could not afford to let these immense resources slip from its grasp.

Lumumba thus had to be brought down, violently if need be. The agency of coercion and repression, the army, was brought into play. However, before finally being pushed on the stage, one final effort was to be made to salvage the situation.

The Loi Fundamentale laid down the rules as to how constitutional authority was to be transferred from the Belgians to the Congolese. The King was invested with the power to appoint a 'formateur' who would then form the government. This power was delegated to Ganshof van der Meerch, the Minister who was there on the spot. This representative of the Belgian monopolies had in his possession not only the known results of the National Assembly, but also knew just how each party fared in the polls. From this knowledge there would have been no question about which person should be approached first and foremost. It would have been Lumumba, not only because his party had the largest number of seats, not only because it was the only one truly national party, but also because it had polled the most number of votes. But then Ganshof was not there to implement the will and desires of the Congolese people, but rather to promote the interests of the Belgian bourgeoisie. He therefore refused to hand over the role of a formateur to Lumumba. Secretly he egged on the puppet parties to come together to form a government. Before the elections, the Minister had said that the administration was counting on the PNP. The people rejected this party of the Belgians and the reactionary chiefs outright, particularly in Orientale province where its reputed strength was pitted to prevent the MNC being returned. Here it was routed. Its leader, Paul Bolya, was defeated and had to enter parliament through the Senate as a representative of UNIMO. Ileo and Adoula, two renegades from the MNC, could not stand on their own platform of Kalondji and entered as UNIMO and Independent respectively. All this showed that this coterie of diehards, stooges and puppets had no support amongst the people. When it came to forming a government PNP could only muster support from PUNA and KALONDJI. Lumumba exposed this dirty trafficking of the Belgian Minister in a Press Conference: 'It would be a crime against the country not to denounce publicly the manoeuvres being carried out by the Belgian Government. Messrs Ileo and Bolkango are being promoted, and we who have the confidence of the people are being pushed aside.'

The action of Ganshof antagonized many people hitherto in opposition to the MNC. They said that according to the rules, Lumumba should be approached. Pressure began to mount that there should be no delay, and as a result, Ganshof appointed Lumumba as informateur. It was therefore his task to inform the Belgian Government as to whether he would be able to form a national government. This was another despicable trick to keep Lumumba out and to give the Belgians more time.

However, on 21 June 1960, the National Assembly met, and the candidates put forward by the Lumumba block decisively routed the Belgian-backed coalition candidates. Joseph Kasongo of the MNC defeated Bolkango of PUNA by 74 votes to 58, for Presidency of the Chamber. The two Vice-Presidencies went to Lumumba candidates. The Belgians and their puppets thus were not only defeated at the polls but also in the Chamber. There had been no alternative but for Ganshof to appoint Lumumba as form-ateur, for in the trial of strength the puppets again failed to rise to the occasion. On 23 June the first nationally elected government was formed in the Congo, with Lu-mumba as its first prime minister.

Many honestly believed that the decades of semi-slavery, barbarism and savagery had at last come to an end. They believed that they as a people, of a country ruthlessly pil-laged and plundered, were on the threshold of a new life where as a free people they would be able to capture their country's former greatness and glory, and play their role in the comity of independent nations. But independence just brought the clash of the forces of revolution and counter-revolution to a head.

13

LUMUMBA IS VICTORIOUS

THOMAS CARLYLE has said that a great man is a beginner precisely because he sees further than others and desires things more strongly than others. But such people however talented, farsighted, however heroic their actions, cannot alter the general trend of historical development. However, what they can do is to alter individual features of events. It is from this participation, from this interaction of possibilities that leaders and great men arise.

The ushering in of the capitalist mode of production brought into society the modern proletariat. At a time when the ideologists of the ruling class were singing hymns to this new order, extolling its superiority over the old, there came on the historical stage Karl Marx. He saw through this new order, exposed its contradictions, and not only saw its destruction as inevitable, but also desired and worked towards that end. As a man, he became a hero to the modern proletariat. It is because of this that the bourgeoisie did all to destroy him, short of assassination. Frederick Engels, Marx's companion in arms, speaking at his graveside said: 'Marx was the best hated and most calumniated man of his time. Governments both absolute and republican deported him from their territories. Bourgeoisie, whether conservative or ultra-democratic, vied with one another to heap slanders upon him. All this he brushed aside as though it were cobweb, ignoring it, answering only when extreme necessity compelled him.'[44]

Lumumba, like Marx, had vision and passionately desired to change the social order; though unlike Marx, he was not fully aware of the workings of historical forces. He too was denigrated, calumniated, and was an object of unbridled venom and abuse from the rulers. He and his ministers were described as 'primitive savages', 'imbeciles' or 'Communist creatures'. A Belgian director of companies in the Congo said on the eve of independence that he hoped to see Lumumba liquidated by a bullet through his head: 'I would be pleased to discover in one of the insane asylums in the Kasai a mad man who would carry out this work.'[45]

This vituperation against Lumumba is understandable. He had a streak, found in many a revolutionary. Engels speaking of Marx said: 'Fighting was his element. And he fought with a passion, tenacity and success such as few could reveal.' So it was too with Lumumba. After 1958, he rose to meet the challenge of the imperialist system and he fought with a tenacity, passion and doggedness that can find few peers amongst the leaders of the African nationalist movement.

The rulers had decided to groom certain leaders of national movements. They saw to it that it was these who would step into their shoes after they had departed physically. But there were leaders of the people who dared to oppose the imperialist attempt at duplicity. They were either systematically eliminated, or flung into isolated concentration camps, where they were brainwashed to 'see reason'. In other words, they tried to crush the spirit of the man, and to suck out all revolutionary passion and ideas. If they succeeded, they let him out and then even made him into a prime minister or a president.

But Lumumba, like Nkrumah, challenged the rulers, even though imprisoned. The leader of the MNC faced insuperable odds. There was the pitiless machine of the administration which gave him no peace. There was scheming and plotting by the directors of Big Business operating behind the façade of 'no politics', and these poured millions of francs into the coffers of puppet parties. Then there were the packs of snarling human hyenas who continually snapped at Lumumba's heels. He had also to face tribalism, regionalism and conservatism from amongst certain layers of the Congolese people.

But Lumumba understood that the people were longing for a change, and he came to tell them that it was possible to bring about that change if they as a nation stood together and demanded independence. With this artillery, which made no concession to backwardness, he broke down the fortresses of conservatism and reaction.

Like Nkrumah and Sékou Touré, Lumumba, in entering the election battle was fighting on a plane which favoured the bourgeoisie. But he beat them. By this time he had lost the inferiority complex which accepted that the Belgians were superior and could not be dislodged. In this respect, he was ahead of many of his contemporaries and colleagues, who still suffered from an inferiority complex even after independence.

The bourgeoisie of Belgium disliked Lumumba, but they had to admit that he had the qualities of a leader. He was dynamic, and the people liked him. In the Council of Ministers, Lumumba was said to be entirely dominant. Most of the ministers respected his brilliance, his capacity for hard work, and his ability to get results. Most of them were afraid of him, and few could stand up to him in argument.

The fact is that the rulers tried in vain to project a leader who would be able to stand up to Lumumba. They tried Ileo, who though trusted was essentially a committee man, good at intrigue, but like a blind worm, completely helpless to face the glare of the sun in broad daylight. At one stage Ganshof, in desperation, tried to appoint Cyrille Adoula as formateur. This was rejected because, Adoula although without question one of the best brains in the country, had no electoral support.

Failing with Ileo and Adoula, they turned to Tshombe. In him they found a man who had no principles whatever, completely shameless, and without dignity or character. As a businessman he was a failure. He was however ambitious. Those who came near him soon learnt that what mattered most to Moise Tshombe was not the country, or people, but Moise Tshombe. To advance his own cause he would go to any lengths, as he did when he placed CONAKAT at the disposal of not only the mining groups, but also the white settlers. Even hardened conservatives kept their distance from him, for in his company they felt that they would be completely exposed to the people.

On the other hand, in the harsh arena of struggle where there were just worms, lackeys and political cut-throats the personality of Lumumba began to flower. Not only did he reveal himself as an organizer and orator, but also as a brilliant tactician. He had acquired a rare flair for gauging the moods of the people. He made shifts here and there, and forged tactical alliances, showing him to be a mature politician despite his comparative youth. He grew in stature in the course of the struggle. With Bolya, Ileo, Adoula, Bolkango, the opposite was the case. Their personalities withered and dried up in the heat of the struggle. The rulers were indeed disappointed that they could not rise up to challenge Lumumba before the people, if not individually, then as a pack. But it could not be otherwise. The rulers had destroyed confidence in themselves when they turned them into lackeys and stooges. In times of action, when speed was required to make decisions, they revealed fatal defects in their personalities. If they could not face the masses it was because they could not take the ideas of the rulers to them, just as they feared to interpret the aspirations of the people for fear of the rulers. Reduced to rodents, they could flourish best in the dark, in the secret recesses of committee meetings.

It had been decided by the Cabinet, of which Lumumba was the Prime Minister, that only one Congolese, namely Kasavubu, should reply to King Baudouin of Belgium, who had arrived to hand over the documents legalizing the transfer of power. The monarch was completely out of touch with the new mood and consciousness of the people and he made an arrogant speech antagonizing all those present. Even those sympathetic to Belgian imperialism admitted that it was paternalistic in the extreme.

The King declared: 'The independence of the Congo is the crowning of the work conceived by the genius of King Leopold II, undertaken by him with courage and continued by Belgium with perserverance. For eighty years Belgium has sent to your land the best of her sons – first to deliver the Congo basin from the odious slave trade which was decimating the population, later to bring together the different tribes which, though former enemies, are now preparing to form the greatest of the Independent States of Africa ... Belgian pioneers have built railways, cities, industries, schools, medical services, and modernized agriculture ... It is your task, gentlemen, to show that we were right in trusting you. The dangers before you are the inexperience of people to govern themselves, tribal fights which have done so much harm, and must at all costs be stopped, and the attraction which some of your regions can have for foreign powers which are ready to profit from the least sign of weakness.'[46]

The King's speech united all the parties in the Chamber. It alienated the moderate ABAKO leadership, and even elements of CONAKAT. The Congolese were angry, for it seemed the King had come to the Congo to whitewash Belgium's bloody record, and to insult them by saying that they were unfit to rule, and to admonish them as if they were children. Furthermore, the King had stated that independence had been graciously *bestowed* by the Belgians, and not *won* by the Congolese people.

Kasavubu dropped the latter portion of his speech, which was meant to be a glowing tribute to the King. And then Lumumba rose to reply.

The sensitive Lumumba was furious that even at this last hour the Belgians should take this occasion to humiliate the Congolese people, and to extol the bloody record of their rule. The King and the Belgian rulers had to be told some stark truths. Lumumba did just that. Before him he saw not the monarch, endowed with the divine right of kings, but just a man. And man to man, Lumumba blasted the King and Belgium's dark and gory record.

He said:

Men and women of the Congo, who have fought for and won the Independence we celebrate today, I salute you in the name of the Congolese Government.

I ask you all, friends who have fought unrelentingly side by side to make this 30th of June, 1960 an illustrious date that remains ineradicably engraved on your hearts, a date whose significance you will be proud to teach to your children, who will in turn pass on to their children and grandchildren the glorious story of our struggle for liberty.

For while the independence of the Congo has today been proclaimed in agreement with Belgium, a friendly country with whom we deal on an equal footing, no Congolese worthy of the name will ever be able to forget that that independence has only been won by struggle, a struggle that went on day after day, a struggle of fire and idealism, a struggle in which we have spared neither effort, deprivation, suffering or even our blood.

This struggle, involving tears, fire and blood, is something of which we are proud in our deepest hearts, for it was a noble and just struggle, which was needed to bring to an end the humiliating slavery imposed on us by force.

Such was our lot for eighty years under the colonialist régime; our wounds are still too fresh and painful for us to be able to forget them at will, for we have experienced painful labour demanded of us in return for wages that were not enough to enable us to eat properly, nor to be decently dressed or sheltered, nor to bring up our children as we longed to.

We have experienced contempt, insults and blows, morning, noon and night, because we were 'blacks'. We shall never forget that a black was called *tu*, not because he was a friend, but because only the whites were given the honour of being called *vous*.

We have seen our lands despoiled in the name of so-called legal documents which were no more than a recognition of superior force.

We have known that the law was never the same for a white man as it was for a black: for the former it made allowances, for the latter it was cruel and inhuman.

We have seen the appalling suffering of those who had their political opinions and religious beliefs dismissed; as exiles in their own country their lot was truly worse than death.

We have seen magnificent houses in the towns for the whites, and crumbling straw huts for the blacks; a black could not go to the cinema, or a restaurant, or a shop that was meant for 'Europeans'; a black would always travel in the lowest part of a ship, under the feet of the whites in their luxurious cabins.

And finally, who can ever forget the firing in which so many of our brothers died; or the cells where those who refused to submit any longer to the rule of a 'justice' of oppression and exploitation were put away?

All this, brothers, has meant the most profound suffering.

But all this, we can now say, we who have been voted by your elected representatives to govern our beloved country, we who have suffered in body and mind from colonialist oppression, all this is now ended.

The Republic of the Congo has been proclaimed, and our land is now in the hands of her own children.

Together, brothers and sisters, we shall start on a new struggle, a noble struggle that will bring our country to peace, prosperity and greatness.

Together, we shall establish social justice, and ensure that everyone is properly rewarded for the work he does.

We shall show the world what the black man can do when he is allowed to work in freedom, and we shall make the Congo the focal point of all Africa.

We shall take care that the soil of our country really provides for the good of her children.

We shall review all the laws of the past, and make new ones that are just and noble.

We shall put an end to all suppression of free thought, and make it possible for all our citizens to enjoy to the full those fundamental freedoms spoken of in the Declaration of Human Rights.

We shall effectively suppress all discrimination of every kind, and give everyone his true place as dictated by his human dignity, his work and his dedication to his country.

We shall set up a rule of peace – not with guns and bayonets, but peace of heart and goodwill.

And for all this, my dear fellow-citizens, you may be sure that we can count not only on our great forces and immense resources but on the aid of many other countries whose collaboration we shall always accept when it is sincere and not an attempt to force us into any political alignment.

In this connection, even Belgium, who, having at last understood the way history was going, has no longer tried to prevent our independence, is ready to give us aid and friendship, and a treaty to that effect has just been signed as between two equal and independent countries. Such cooperation, I am sure, will profit both our countries. For our part, while remaining on the watch, we shall respect the engagements into which we have freely entered.

Thus, both within and without, the new Congo which my government creates will be a rich, free, and prosperous country. But if we are to achieve this object quickly, I must ask you all, legislators and citizens of the Congo, to do everything in your power to help me.

I ask you all to forget the tribal rivalries that dissipate our energies and make us the laughing-stock of foreigners.

I ask the parliamentary minority to help my government by making their opposition constructive and keeping it strictly within legal and democratic channels.

I ask you all to hold back from no sacrifice that will ensure the success of our magnificent enterprise.

Lastly, I ask you to show unconditional respect for the lives and goods both of your fellow-citizens and of the foreigners living in our midst.

If those foreigners behave badly, they will be expelled from our territory by law; if, on the other hand, they behave well, then they must be left in peace, for they too are working for the good of the Congo.

The independence of the Congo marks a decisive step towards the liberation of the whole African continent.

This, then, Your Majesty, Your Excellencies, Ladies and Gentlemen, my dear fellow-citizens, my brothers by blood, and my brothers in the struggle, this is what I wanted to say to you in the name of the government on this wonderful day of our full and sovereign independence.

Our government, strong, national and popular, will be the salvation of this country.

I urge all Congolese citizens, men, women and children, to set resolutely to work to create a prosperous national economy and thus guarantee our economic independence.

Honour to those who have fought for national liberty!

Long live the independence and unity of Africa!

Long live the sovereign and independent Congo!

Lumumba's speech was warmly applauded and he was persuaded to cyclostyle it and to send it throughout the Congo. This was done.

Many of the representatives of the people must have been similarly angered on independence day when the colonial power glorified its so-called achievements. But the replies of the leaders of the national movements were different, although they felt the same as Lumumba did. Lumumba thus spoke openly, and what was in his mind, not only for the people of the Congo but for the people of the entire continent of Africa. For in his indictment of Belgian rule, he equally indicted the sordid and bloody colonial record of British, French, Portuguese and Spanish imperialism in Africa.

14

COUNTER REVOLUTIONARY REVOLT BY UNION MINIÈRE

WHAT has been described as the secession of Katanga Province from the Congo was in reality a counter revolutionary revolt engineered by Union Minière and the big monopolies operating in the Congo. It was backed to the hilt by the Belgian Government. If its African mouthpiece, CONAKAT shifted its stand from secession to federalism and vice versa, it was only because it was keeping its options open. If there had been a victory of the puppet parties, or if Lumumba had given some sign that he was going to soften as a result of attaining high office, then there would have been federalism. But with Lumumba in their eyes being intransigent, and at the helm in the centre, monopoly capital struck from its base area, Katanga, which now proclaimed its independence.

Katanga is the most industrialized province in the Congo. At independence it absorbed 22 per cent of Congo's machinery, 77 per cent of its rail freight goods, 61 per cent of the tobacco, 32 per cent of electrical apparatus, 40 per cent of textiles, 38 per cent of its meat, 26 per cent of its paper, 42 per cent of its power and explosives, and 35 per cent of its chemical products. Towering and casting its dark ominous shadow over the whole of the Congo, as well as Katanga, was the Union Minière, subsidiary of the Société Générale. The shares of Union Minière as at 1960, before independence, were divided as follows:

Shareholder	Number of shares	%
TC (Tanganyika Concessions)	179,760	14·5
SG (Société Générale)	57,685	4·6
CSK (Katanga Special Committee)	315,675	25·4
CK (Compagnie du Katanga)	18,500	1·5
Others: French, Belgian and small holdings	670,380	54·0

The significant holding was the CSK (Katanga Special Committee). TC (Tanganyika Concessions), and also referred to as TANKS, was a British Company. Union Minière represented a consortium of Belgian, British and French capitalists. The CSK though holding only 25·4 per cent of the shares had however 35·7 per cent of the voting rights.

However, just before independence, the CSK mysteriously dissolved and its shares were divided, giving two-thirds to the Congo Government, and one-third to the Compagnie du Katanga. The position of the shareholding was as follows:

Shareholder	% of holding
Congo government	23·82
TC	20·21
CK	12·96
SG	6·94
Others	36·13

This was outright theft by the big monopolies, and also it was a ganging up to surround the Lumumba Government. Prior to this robbery, the Belgian Government was in a key position by its voting strength of over 37 per cent, to outvote any of the monopolies should the interests clash at any time. It was not so with the Congolese Government which could now be outvoted. But even this arrangement, though inequitable, was never implemented, for when Tshombe declared Katanga independent, the monopolists stole the entire assets of the CSK which, by virtue of independence, would belong entirely to the government of the Congo. This money was surely needed to stabilize the finances of the government. There is no doubt that Lumumba would not have tolerated this theft which was so open and blatant. There is little doubt he would have called the Union Minière to give an account of this outrageous behaviour. But the bourgeoisie struck before this happened, and declared their UDI (Unilateral Declaration of Independence).

Undoubtedly, this was an extreme step, but there was no alternative. Just as the Belgian Government tried to keep the MNC out of the government machinery by legal subterfuges, so too, the monopolies made one more effort to take control of the central government. CONAKAT which had won only eight seats in the National Assembly, representing only a small tribe in Katanga, now demanded the ministries of Defence and Interior. The MNC and the other parties regarded these demands as outrageous and an insult to the people who had rejected CONAKAT so completely. Yet there was distinct logic in the demands of CONAKAT. Union Minière, Forminière, Cotonco, the HCB (subsidiary of Unilever), some of the largest of the monopolists, controlled 90 per cent of the Congo's trade. Monopoly capital thus was the dominant economic organization in the Congo and was demanding the right to control the leading apparatus of coercion and suppression, the army and the police. That is why they went for the key ministries. The MNC and the other parties would have no truck with this and the plan was rejected.

Political power by Lumumba's government at the centre and in some of the provinces, and economic control by Union Minière and the other monopolists were bound to be incompatible. If both were moving from their political positions as a result of pressures from their respective forces, then sooner or later they would confront one another. In this confrontation, one had to go. Therefore before Lumumba had time to consolidate, the monopolists struck and declared Katanga independent.

The secession was part of a wide plan, and the paper *France Observateur* published this sinister scheme a week later, after 14 July 1960, the date of the UDI of Katanga. It said: 'Operation Katanga is not aimed at detaching a rich province from the rest of a poor country, but aimed at re-grouping around Mr Tshombe, the creature of Union Minière, the maximum loyal provinces, Kivu, where the majority of the settlers live, Ruanda Urundi, Kalondji's Kasai, and even Equatorial Province. It is not so much the splitting up of the Congo that these circles intend, as its recreation around another axis than the Leopoldville axis around Lumumba.' The whole strategy of the monopolists was to pit the puppet régimes against the government based on the power of the people.

The mining monopolies were not wholly owned by the Belgians. At the time of independence, the *Financial Times*, organ of British financiers stated that an informed estimate predicted that TANKS would control 21 per cent of the votes of Union Minière. TANKS was British and three of its directors sat as directors of Union Minière. America came in not only through the control of the banking system but also through the acquisition by Rockerfeller of certain important shares. The *Financial Times* went on to say that a new factor in the position of Société Générale came from its recent alliance with the Rockerfeller group. The latter's Congo holdings were to be transferred to a subsidiary of the Société Générale in which Rockerfeller would be allotted shares of a nominal value of 65 million francs. This then was the economic basis for the internationalization of the question of the secession of Katanga. That is why all the imperialist powers were vitally concerned, because their investments were directly involved. Further, imperialism was also concerned about what would happen to the Congo, because of its importance as a producer of strategic raw materials. The following Table shows the relative importance of the Congo's minerals in comparison with the total production in Africa, in 1953.

Mineral	% of production
Cobalt	86
Diamonds	64
Silver	51
Copper	34
Tin	60
Tungsten	53

Then there was uranium, and a secret agreement was made by Union Minière with the USA to supply this ore.

Imperialism is prepared to go to war if necessary to prevent it being deprived of its profits, and also of its strategic war materials. To protect this life blood it will not hesitate to create chaos, render a country bankrupt, and flatten it with merciless bombing to achieve its ends. It did just that in the Congo. But imperialism was planning to go further. It was prepared to plunge the whole of central and southern Africa into an arena of white-black confrontation, bringing in the oppressors of South Africa, if the situation could not be contained.

The Congo was a valuable prize for any imperialist power. They fought amongst themselves for this prize, but first they all united to destroy Lumumba and the revolutionary forces round him. The forces of secession engineered by the forces of counter revolution two weeks after the independence of the Congo, ushered in the new phase of the attempted imperialist reconquest of Africa. This was to go hand in hand with the process of granting flag independence. Belgium gave independence to the Congo on 30 June 1960, and by her actions two weeks later took it away through the secession of Katanga. The life and death struggle between the forces of revolution and counter revolution which is now raging in intensity in the seventies, had begun in the Congo a decade earlier. The first shots were fired when the traitor Tshombe declared his Katangan UDI.

15

THE UN TROJAN HORSE
ENTERS THE CONGO

ON the eve of independence, a treaty of friendship between Belgium and the Congo was signed to the effect that the former was to intervene militarily only at the request of the latter. But when Belgian troops flew into Elizabethville, the capital of Katanga, to give military backing to the secession of Katanga, not only was this aggression, but it was a violation of a treaty on which the ink had hardly dried. Lumumba alerted the Congolese nation to this new danger when he said: 'We have learnt that the Belgian Government has sent troops to the Congo, and they have intervened. The responsibility of the Belgian Government is great. We protest bitterly against these measures which prejudice good relations between our countries. We appeal to all Congolese to defend our Republic against those who threaten it. Between 10 to 18 July over 10,000 Belgian troops occupied 23 places, showing that the reoccupation of the Congo had been a calculated and planned affair.'

Within two weeks, the new government was faced with a series of strikes by workers, mutiny among the Force Publique, the secession of Katanga, and the re-coccupation of the Congo by Belgium. The first two problems were not insurmountable and Lumumba's personal intervention solved them, particularly after his firm undertaking that he would Africanize the army including the top command. The latter two problems, both connected, were of a different kind, for it was counter revolution which was now on the attack.

The chaos into which the Congo was plunged must be seen against the background of the sudden deterioration of the economic position of the Congo. The Belgians, as expected, left the country bankrupt, having drained away all they could. Seldom even in the history of modern colonization, known for its rapacious plunder, has one seen such naked, ruthless and savage plunder of a country so rich in natural and human resources as the Congo. In the five years preceding independence there was a net outflow of £464 million pounds. In 1958, Union Minière made a clean profit of £28 million. But on the eve of independence the Congo was saddled with a public debt of £300 million. This amounted to the payment of 17 per cent of the expenses of the ordinary budget, and this would increase to 24·2 per cent in 1960.

The US *News and World Report,* no friend of Lumumba and the organ of American millionaires however said: 'Surplus earned for Belgium averaged 200 million a year. This included 80 million of shipping and insurance and 60 million in dividends and interest. ... These are substantial sums for a small nation of fewer than 10 million.' The position Belgium left the independent Congo in economically can be seen by the following table:

BUDGET FIGURES FOR THE CONGO
(in million francs)

	Credits	*Debits*	*Balance*
1948	5,223	4,698	524
1951	8,012	6,355	1,657
1955	10,730	9,496	1,223
1957	11,676	12,260	−584

In 1958 the deficit rose to 2 billion francs or 40 million dollars. In 1960 the deficit was to rise to 6 billion francs or to 120 million dollars.

And if this was not enough, the Belgian Minister Raymond Scheyven pushed through with Congolese consent two further loans of £14 million pounds from the World Bank and another £7 million from the American Finance Corporation. These were at normal rates of interest of 6 per cent payable over five years. The Belgians made a great show by the offer of £19 million pounds as a 'gift' and an undertaking by the Belgian monopolists that they would rapatriate £18 million. These were however just palliatives. The Congo, the young baby, was not only baptized in blood, but it came into the world with economic chains that tied it hand and foot to the monopolies.

Lumumba confidently believed that the Congolese people left to themselves would be able to solve their problems. He flew to Elizabethville with Kasavubu. There they were prevented from landing. In other words, the puppet Godfrey Munongo refused permission to his own President and Prime Minister to land. This was treason, but then this servile creature received a pat on the back from his white master when Major Weber congratulated Munongo for 'his performance at the airport'.

It was then that Lumumba appealed to the United Nations for help to oust the invaders. The Security Council met and passed the following resolution. The Security Council:

1. confirms the authority given to the Secretary General by the Security Council resolutions of 14 July and 22 July 1960 and requests him to continue to carry out the responsibility placed on him thereby;
2. calls upon the government of Belgium to withdraw immediately its troops from the Province of Katanga under speedy modalities determined by the Secretary General and to assist in every possible way the implementation of the Council's resolutions;
3. declares that the entry of the United Nations Force into the Province of Katanga is necessary for the full implementation of this resolution;
4. reaffirms that the United Nations Force in the Congo will not be a party to or in any way intervene in or influence the outcome of any internal conflict, constitutional or otherwise;
5. calls upon all Member States, in accordance with 25 and 49 of the Charter of the United Nations, to accept and carry out the decisions of the Security Council and

to afford mutual assistance in carrying out measures decided upon by the Council;

6. requests the Secretary General to implement this resolution and to report further to the Council as appropriate.

The United Nations, normally slow and lethargic when it comes to protecting the interests of the oppressed against aggression, was quick in the case of the Congo. By 25 July 1960, the UN had in the Congo a force of 8,396 officers and men, of which 2340 were Ghanaians, 2087 Tunisians, 1220 Moroccans, 1160 Ethiopians, 741 Guineans, 623 Swedes and 225 Liberians. The Ghanaians and Swedes were in Leopoldville, the Tunisians in Kasai, the Ethiopians in Orientale. Liberian, Ethiopian, and Moroccan detachments were in Equator, and it was planned to send the Irish battalion to Kivu as soon as it arrived.

What was surprising was that the UN troops moved into all the provinces *except* Katanga. In other words, they took over and occupied the very provinces where they were not required and where their services were not needed, or requested. They refused to enter Katanga where they were supposed to go to help the Congo Government to dislodge the rebel régime.

It was obvious then that the United Nations armed forces came not to liberate the province of Katanga from the aggressors, but to occupy the Congo under the control of the Lumumba Government. Thus the new Republic had within a month of its existence two armies of occupation, one in the form of the old rulers, who were open and unashamed aggressors, and the other an invited army which turned out to be a Trojan horse. Just what, and who he let in, Lumumba learnt the bitter and hard way. The 'friends' soon dropped their masks and showed their true colours. Lumumba was trapped between two armies, the UN in some respects being the more insidious because it had Africans in it. Lumumba had now to fight not only against them but also against his illusions about the nature of the UN troops which were composed mostly of African contingents.

If there was one mistake that Lumumba made in his political career, which cost him his life, it was to invite the UN to the Congo. But it was the mistake of the whole of Africa, both radical and conservative. It was the mistake of the Accra Conference of 1958 as well as of socialist countries to foster the illusion that the UN assisted the liberation of oppressed people. In fact the opposite was the case. The UN was in the pocket of imperialism, especially US imperialism, and was instrumental in fostering the neocolonialist policies of the imperialist powers. Only the South African based Unity Movement of South Africa had at that stage analysed the United Nations and had taken up a position which defended the interests of the colonial masses. It saw the UN as a continuation of the League of Nations, which had discredited itself over its failure to stop the Italian aggression in Abyssinia, and which had allowed the growth of Italian and German Fascism which cost the lives of millions of people. There were new faces in the United Nations. There were more African and Asian nations, but its essential character did not change from that of the old League of Nations. It was still the instrument of imperialism with most of the new African and Asian states consciously, or unconsciously, serving its interests.

The whole of the Congo was up in arms at the invasion of the Belgians, but this was not the case when UN troops arrived. In fact the UN troops were amazed at the reception they met. A correspondent was pleasantly surprised at the reception of Moroccan troops. He said: 'They met with no resistance. Instead, station officials turned out to welcome them at the wayside, and crowds poured on to platforms cheering and offering huge bunches of bananas to the troops ... the rebel soldiers (Congolese) were as vociferous in their welcome as the civilian crowds.' The deception then that they were liberators had worked. Only after they had begun their deadly work was it realized that they had let in enemies disguised as friends.

Instead of moving into Katanga, the UN decided to establish what they called 'law and order'. This they did by disarming the Congolese soldiers. They also made concerted moves to 'imprison' them by calling on the soldiers to return to their barracks. This was done not only without the permission of the Congolese Government, but against its wishes.

In Leopoldville, this task of disarming the troops fell on the Ghanaian troops. In one case, Brigadier Otu, one of the senior officers in the Ghanaian army was seen personally disarming a Congolese soldier, with the Belgians present clapping. Lumumba summoned Otu and stated in clear terms that he would not tolerate the further disarming of his troops, and that it had to stop. But it continued all the same. It was clear that the troops were obeying an outside power which though invisible, was nevertheless pulling the strings. However, what this action on the part of the UN meant, was that it deprived Lumumba of the only possible internal force that would be capable of dislodging the Belgians. This gave the Tshombe régime valuable time to consolidate its hold.

Lumumba had made the request to the UN in the firm belief that the troops were to be under the command of the legitimate government of the country. The Security Council resolution also gave that impression, for no action was to be taken except with the consultation of Lumumba's Government. But on arrival, the UN troops behaved as if they were an army of occupation. They began to collaborate with the Belgians, and behaved as if the government of Lumumba did not exist.

Gizenga, the Vice-Premier, told the Secretary General, Dag Hammarskjold rather bluntly: 'The people of the Congo do not understand that we, against whom aggression has been committed, we who are in our land, we who have made an appeal to international armed forces are systematically and methodically disarmed, while the aggressors, the Belgians, who are here in a conquered territory, still have their arms and the power of death and are simply being asked to go to certain parts of the Congo which some dare call Belgian bases.'

In the earlier period, Lumumba believed that it was Ralphe Bunche, and later Hammarskjold who were responsible for this state of affairs. Later, he began to understand that the UN itself was being manipulated by certain invisible forces.

Clashes took place between the UN and the Congolese troops, and Lumumba realized that it would be better to fight it out alone, remarking: 'We are ready to renounce the services of UN troops.' Earlier, he had called for the withdrawal of all white troops.

The UN invasion can only be understood if one is able to lay bare the inner mechanism of this Trojan horse, and just who were its invisible charioteers, and its passengers. In other words, one must lay bare the hidden hand of US imperialism in this dark and shameful history of the Congo Republic.

16

THE HIDDEN HAND OF US IMPERIALISM IN THE CONGO

THE question that one may ask is how was it possible for US imperialism not only to manipulate the United Nations, but also to deceive the African States? At one stage even Lumumba appealed to the US for direct aid. The answer lies in the fact that the USA did not have a colonial record in Africa, unlike the European powers. The USA did not join in the scramble for Africa, nor did it take a major share in the carve up of the world. But on the other hand, it had States which were utterly dependent on it. Lenin in his 'Imperialism' said that 'typical of this epoch were not only the two main groups of countries, those owning colonies, but also the diverse forms of dependent countries, which officially were politically independent, but in fact were enmeshed in financial and diplomatic dependence. He further added: 'Finance capital is such a great, it may be said, such a decisive force, in all economic international relations, that it is capable of actually subjecting even the States enjoying the fullest political independence.'

American hegemony was clearly established in Latin America after World War II, and so decisive is its pull due to its economic power that it can make and unmake governments in that sub-continent. It may be said that some of the Presidents in Latin American countries are on the payroll of the monopolist combines operating there.

The end of World War II saw the former European colonial powers utterly exhausted, and dependent on handouts from America. So strong was the dollar that it was as valuable as gold. American imperialist interests demanded that the former colonies which had hitherto remained closed to the penetration of American capital be opened up to it. It suited the interests of US imperialism if the colonies became politically independent, because then the US could be on an equal footing with the excolonial power. So on this point the interest of American imperialism coincided with those national liberation movements which wanted political independence. The US monopolists stood to end the old style colonialism which involved the upkeep of large colonial armies which were expensive to maintain. In the era of the awakening of the masses these armies in any event would not be able to stem the revolutionary tides. Thus the US projected itself as a champion of the colonial peoples and their aspirations. It could indeed afford to be very liberal on that score because it had no colonies of its own to sacrifice. In its propaganda in the colonies, and former colonies, it was never tired of drawing attention to the fact that it also had a colonial past, and that it overthrew Britain's oppressive rule in 1776. Therefore in Africa, the US projected the image of a liberator. A writer details how the US worked as regards this continent: 'The US is inescapably committed to a moderate and a responsible policy towards Africa. Our government brings pressure to bear through diplomatic persuasion, and through votes on African issues in the UN; through the Voice of America and other propaganda media; through our education exchange programme and technical assistance to Africa.'[47]

The reaction of the older imperial powers to this new look of America was further given by the author when he added:

'The mingled irritation and uneasiness of American pressure is well reflected in the attitude of Andre Seigfried who once suggested that the US, by fomenting colonial revolts, was as dangerous a revolutionary force as the Soviet Union.' But behind all this rhetoric and bombast was the stark reality that the US wanted a place in the sun in the colonies, even if it meant ousting a colonial power. In the case of the Congo, it decided on the latter course, not only because of the high return on its investment, but also because the Congo contained two vital strategic raw materials, uranium and cobalt. It was the Congo that provided the raw material that made it possible to manufacture the atomic bomb which was dropped on Hiroshima in Japan in 1945.

American capital had entered the Congo at the dawn of the twentieth century. But by the time of independence it had moved into this country in a big way. A great deal of prominence has been given to one Detwiler, who reputedly representing American bankers and businessmen, concluded a 2 billion dollar deal to supply technical personnel to the Congo. However, more significant, precisely because it was done more discreetly and showed the workings of the real financiers, was the action of the American-dominated World Bank, which gave a loan of £14 million and another £7 million from a group of American financiers. This was apart from the loan which Belgium received from America for its £350 million Ten-Year Development programme. There was a stiff rate of interest of 6 per cent, and the loan was to be repaid by 1978.

Such was the power and strength of American monopoly capital that through the acquisition of shares in Société Générale, the Rockefellers and Morgans took control of the Congo Central Bank. The significance of this move lay in the fact that it was this bank which controlled all foreign transactions. So even if Britain, France and Belgium controlled the visible assets like the mines, industries, and plantations, it was the Americans who controlled finance. And it is finance capital in this age of super monopoly capital which, when paying the piper, also calls the tune.

If American policy was to oust Belgium, this was reflected

in the economic field. Belgium had lost grip. That is why observers noted a difference in America's policy towards Britain and France on the one hand, and Belgium on the other. In the case of the former, it cooperated with these powers towards evolving political policies to achieve freedom, but in the Congo this policy was reversed. The US Government appeared to by-pass the Belgian Government as much as possible and to deal directly with the Congolese Government on economic, fiscal, and technical aid programmes, or to funnel such aid through the UN and other international agencies.

But before the US could pursue its policy fully, one obstacle had to be removed – Lumumba. The US planners sized him up when he visited the UN, and later stayed in the Presidential Lodge. They saw he was too dedicated and earnest to be relied upon to protect their interests. This view was confirmed when Lumumba saw the Soviet Ambassador in Ottawa. Thus US imperialism decided that a united Front must be formed to liquidate Lumumba. What could then be a better instrument than that of the UN troops of African States which Lumumba himself had invited into the Congo?

The difference then between the Belgians and the Americans was that while the former had to work through discredited people like Tshombe, the latter had the services of African countries which had been placed in a position to tie Lumumba's hands.

In the UN Assembly, or even in the Security Council, imperialism is attacked and these assemblies pass radical resolutions. The condemnation of Belgian aggression was one such resolution. But the actual implementation was left to the Secretariat, and it was here that US imperialism had a firm grip. In August 1960, most of the senior posts in the Secretariat were held by America and its imperialist allies. When Lumumba called upon the UN, Hammarskjold was surrounded by a ring of US advisers. These were Ralphe Bunche, Under Secretary for political affairs, and his personal representative in the Congo, Heinz Wenshoff, Bunche's deputy. Andrew Cordier was executive assistant.

This was apart from Hammarskjold's own connection with the Belgian royal family. They were thus at times at odds with Lumumba, because through the UN machinery they had to carry out American aims.

On the military side, the penetration was deadlier, as swarms of men disguised as advisers and experts moved in to the Congo. They went straight for Lumumba's army, sometimes with his own blessing. However, one person whom Lumumba clashed with was General Alexander. He was the Chief of Staff of the armed forces of Ghana, but in the Congo he did not head any Ghanaian contingent. Neither did he have an official position in the UN team. Yet he was constantly referred to as 'commander'. This Colonel Blimp did not disguise his aim, which was to smash the Force Publique under the pretext of restoring law and order, and to render Lumumba completely harmless and ineffective.

With the swarm of invaders flew in also the CIA. It is one of the unwritten conditions attached to every US 'aid' or loan that it admits the CIA. In typical fashion CIA men set to work, tempting, corrupting and bribing the Congolese leaders. With a budget of 2 billion dollars, more than the budget of any of the Independent States of Africa, it had dollars to give away. Tshombe it did not bother to corrupt for he had already put himself up for sale. Rather they looked for new and untried elements, who had leading positions in the government. One person they singled out for special favour was Joseph Mobutu, for he was to be the Chief of Staff, second only to the Commander.

Mobutu grew up in the MNC. Lumumba trusted him as one of the younger cadres who would play an important role in the future of the nation. He was brought into Lumumba's first Cabinet as junior minister although he had no place in the National Assembly. Later, Lumumba put him in charge of building the Congolese army the Armée Nationale Congolaise (ANC). The only man above Mobutu was Lundula, who was the Commander in Chief. The CIA found out that besides being a soldier, Mobutu was a journalist before he joined the army. Mobutu, then, during his period as junior minister was with Lumumba ministries. In that sense he was one of the inner trusted group. The CIA were therefore very happy with their find for who could be better than Mobutu who grew up under Lumumba, and knew the inner workings of the MNC? Tulley in his book on the CIA *The CIA: The Inside Story*, says that Mobutu was 'discovered' by the CIA. Paul W. Blackstock, a political scientist at the University of South Carolina has also revealed that CIA intervention in the troubled Congo in support of Colonel Mobutu contributed materially to the 'stability' of the régime during the first years of its independence.

Others, particularly ABAKO, were infiltrated by the French. Corruption also took place at a lower level as well, for careerists, political rejects, and hirelings rose from the sewers and the gutters to begin a smear campaign against their own premier. Thus one, Vital Mwanda of ABAKO said: 'If Lumumba is not voted out of office we shall strike by other means, and it will be right on the target. ABAKO intends to rid the country of Lumumba by legal or illegal means.'

In other circumstances Mwanda and his associates would have been swiftly dealt with and charged with incitement and even treason. But now they could say these things freely because they had the protection of their masters. What was being whispered by the Belgians, French, British and US imperialists privately in clubs, was now being spread publicly by these hirelings and puppets. It was aimed at preparing the population for what was to follow.

How many millions of dollars flowed into the Congo is not known, but what was funnelled through the UN is known. The figures show that what was supposed to be a UN force was in fact financed by the US. Between July 1960 to June 1963 American 'aid' to the Congo totalled some 299,649,613 dollars. Of this 118,481,290 (40 per cent) was the American contribution to the cost of the UN force. Congress made readily available to the President of the US another 10 million dollars in case of emergency in the Congo.

Lumumba fought the agents of the US imperialism even if he did not fully know the extent of their involvement. However, by their concrete actions in the Congo, he saw that

145

they were moving in a direction against the spirit of the UN resolutions by by-passing him. He fought all the UN officials at one time or another, whether it was Hammarskjold, Bunche, Cordier, or Alexander. But he could not comprehend the deep ramifications, as well as the links of US imperialism. Against his known and open enemies, he put trust in those whom he believed were loyal and true to the cause, only to find that they had become Judases, who had also sold the honour and the people of the Congo for dollars, and numbered accounts in foreign banks.

17

THE PAN AFRICAN CONFERENCE AT LEOPOLDVILLE

THE oppressed in their long and arduous struggle against exploitation learn hard and bitter lessons through sheer suffering. So too with Lumumba. He learnt from the taunts, arrogance, and humiliations he suffered from leading UN personnel that he had let in invaders who occupied his land under the guise of liberators. Their presence and activities did more to weaken the authority of the central government than the aggression by Belgium. The result was that it helped to strengthen the authority of the puppet Tshombe. Lumumba then told the UN rather bluntly that they must depart, for their services were no longer required.

But Lumumba was in desperate need of genuine and real friends. He turned to Africa, particularly to those countries which were free in his eyes. Therefore, instead of travelling directly to Leopoldville from his US trip, he decided to contact various African Heads of States. His main aim was to mobilize a force outside the UN which would be able to get rid of the Belgian aggressors. Therefore, between the 2nd and 8th of August 1960, he visited Tunisia, Morocco, Guinea, Ghana, Liberia and Togoland. All these countries endorsed the idea of a united Congo and condemned the

146

action of the Belgians. But only in Guinea and Ghana did he get specific commitments, that they were prepared to place their entire armed forces at the disposal of the Congolese Government if the UN did not achieve the evacuation of the invaders. The idea of an African High Command was suggested by Kwame Nkrumah. President Nasser cabled that he supported such a move and also gave Lumumba the backing he desired.

The other countries, however, were hostile to an independent High Command outside the UN. Bourguiba of Tunisia went out of his way to pay tribute to Hammarskjold's handling of the situation, which tied Lumumba's hand by stating that the Secretary General's actions were helping to strengthen peace, security and good relations. This was the language of a puppet typical of the kind which Africa was to see more of in the later part of the decade. In Togoland the UN was also praised 'for the stand taken over the Congo and for measures taken to ensure peace and security'. Lumumba was inexperienced at this type of double-talk, which was meant not for his ears but for those of their masters in Washington and Brussels. One does not know what was discussed in private, but he believed that he scored a triumph when they all agreed to attend a Conference, together with other independent African States to be held in Leopoldville on 25 August 1960.

Lumumba returned to the Congo in high spirits because he believed that at last in Africa he had found real friends, who acting together, would constitute a force to challenge the might of the aggressors. At a press conference he paid more attention to his African allies than to the UN. What helped him in his attitude was that both Nkrumah and Sékou Touré had already informed the UN Secretary General that they were considering putting their troops at the disposal of the Lumumba Government.

The Pan–African Conference opened with the representatives of thirteen independent African States, as well as members of national liberation movements. The States were Cameroon, Congo Brazzaville, Ethiopia, Ghana, Guinea, Liberia, Mali, Morocco, Somalia, Sudan and Togoland. But the composition of the Conference was such as to make any reasonable man despair. Although it was supposed to be a Foreign Ministers' Conference it was attended by ambassadors of African countries accredited locally, or attached to the UN. It was clear that they would not do anything to upset the UN forces in the Congo. What might have been a mountain turned out to be a molehill.

The Conference expressed regret that there was no cooperation between the UN and the Congolese Government but sent a message to Bunche, expressing appreciation of his services. It said also that all aid should be channelled through the UN. Guinea's proposal, that the Conference consider ways and means to overthrow Tshombe's régime was rejected. However, the States said that they could act as negotiators between the Congo Government and the secessionists.

In their speeches, delegates like Mongo Slim of Tunisia, already being groomed by imperialism for bigger things, chastized Lumumba for daring to criticize the Secretary General. Likewise, the behaviour of the Force Publique was attacked, while the action of UN troops in disarming the Congolese soldiers was exonerated and rationalized. Further, the fact that the UN had betrayed the trust put in it, and had violated its own resolutions, was side-stepped, and full praise was heaped upon it.

In reality, with a few exceptions, the Pan-African Conference turned out to be a Conference of 'Tshombes', gathered not to oust their fellow Tshombe, but to decide on the fate of Lumumba. It was the political consciousness of the people of the Congo that created the historical accident that it was Lumumba, and not a Tshombe who was returned to power as the country's first premier. Imperialism was determined not to have another Nkrumah and Sékou Touré in West Africa, and was now scheming to set the clock back and reverse the conquests of the people. Those at the Conference were more interested in ingratiating themselves with their masters than with helping their fellow African in his plight.

How else can one explain the behaviour of these Africans

148

at the Conference? Those who were present did not lack forces. In fact the majority of the UN forces were drawn from the very countries participating in the Conference. Their troops were carrying out orders, one of which was to disarm the Force Publique while allowing the Belgians to get off scot free. African troops were rendering their fellow troops harmless and impotent, while allowing the white troops to retain their arms. Is it small wonder that the US spent over 100 million dollars for the upkeep of the UN force? It is more than likely that the bulk of the money went into the pockets of the top brass amongst African military and civilian personnel.

The Africans were the largest force in the Congo UN contingent, and not a single African was there in the High Command of the United Nations Operational Command (ONUC). The Secretary General on the civilian side was assisted by Sir Alexander McFarquhar and Brigadier Rokhe. Below them were three Americans. Von Horn headed the military side. In other words, in all the major issues, it was these men from the Western countries who made the decisions, and it was the Africans, who were not even consulted, who received instructions to carry them out. Thus we see the spectacle of Africans being used to crush fellow Africans. It was all done under the grandiose phrases of the UN charter.

All support to the UN meant that the Conference rejected the idea of an African High Command. Yet what did the idea of an All-African High Command mean? African governments would make decisions and then it would be their own soldiers who would carry out the decisions. By their resolution to give full aid to the UN they were in effect saying to their masters that they rejected independence for themselves, and preferred tutelage under the UN, or in other words, tutelage under the US and other imperialist powers.

However, it must be conceded that their stand on this reflected the real position, for these Independent States in fact were under varying degrees of tutelage. Politically, they might appear to be free, with their own flags, presidents, parliaments, and prime ministers. But economically they were tied to the apron strings of imperialism. Not only were the commanding heights of the economy in the hands of foreigners, but most of the country was mortgaged to the former colonial powers.

Political independence in fact had placed power in the hands of a tiny section of the propertied classes. They spoke on behalf of the entire people, but in fact served the interests of the African bourgeoisie. Their role in their own countries was not that of free men to give impetus to the productive forces in society, but to guard the interests of the monopolists. Their mentality was that of foremen. The position they took on the question of the Congo, where they had to choose between a fellow African who was in trouble, and their masters, reflected their position at home. Lackeys at home they carried their stamp of abject servility abroad, and hid behind paper documents like the United Nations Charter.

The 1960 Leopoldville Conference was important for here was the independence of a sister country being menaced. It was the first test of the calibre of the national movement which received independence. Just what were its politics, just what was its ideology and what was its position *vis-à-vis* the people and imperialism? Here they showed themselves in their true colours. Far from ranging themselves behind Lumumba they did all they could to demoralize him, and to destroy his confidence that the Belgians could be dislodged.

To many, the Leopoldville Conference was a great blow to the Pan-African cause. Since the Accra Conference of 1958, the idea of Pan-Africanism had grown; but here was its first real challenge. It was all very well voting for resolutions extolling Pan–Africanism, but now imperialism had fired its first shots in its reconquest of the continent. If imperialism succeeded in the Congo, then no really independent country was safe. The issue was that simple.

The Conference revealed two trends in Pan–African politics. One section wanted to move out of the orbit of the former colonial masters, while the other wanted to entrench them in power. This was shown when Guinea, for example, openly sided with Lumumba and wanted to retake Katanga with an African force, while the majority of others vetoed the proposal. The same could be said of Ghana's proposal for an African High Command. It met with the same fate. Both these trends continued to exist and both appeared later in the Organization of African Unity (OAU). The existence of these conflicting sections has paralysed Africa from taking any effective action on every major issue which has confronted it since the beginning of the nineteen-sixties. In this period, more States were given flag independence. Numerically the strength of free Africa increased, but in reality it weakened, for imperialism was able to get in voices to plead on its behalf.

The decade of the sixties was characterized by the achieving of political freedom with the bourgeoisie at the helm. But inevitably, it was a bourgeoisie tied to imperialism. It could not do anything to solve burning problems, for that would have involved struggle against its masters.

The Congo was the beginning of a series of assaults by imperialism on African independence, and free Africa looked on helplessly and exhausted itself in talking, while counter-revolution moved in with guns and artillery and consolidated its hold. After Lumumba, civilian after civilian governments in Africa have been toppled. While the African States lent their armies to US imperialism under the UN, yet they did not send a single one of their soldiers to defend the founder of the OAU, Kwame Nkrumah, when he was driven from power in the reactionary coup in February, 1966. There have also been the cases of Namibia and Rhodesia. In all this one sees the utter failure to get to grips with the problem. It is clear that the task of eliminating imperialism from Africa and of wiping out colonialism must fall on the shoulders of politically-conscious worker and peasant parties committed to socialism.

For Lumumba, the Leopoldville fiasco was another bitter pill to swallow; for another illusion was destroyed. Instead of practical help for his troops or vital supplies, which he sorely needed, he got advice on how he and his soldiers should behave. Instead of getting support on the issue of the perfidious role of the UN, he found delegates at the

Leopoldville Conference queuing up to lavish praise. Mongo Slim actually said that Africa must not allow UN prestige to be damaged in the Congo. Some countries even went to the extent of chastizing the Congolese Government for not allowing the disarming of Congolese troops because of their bad behaviour. Lumumba, who believed that the Leopoldville Conference would get down to the business of discussing specific ways in which Africa could help in providing troops, had to be content to extract an undertaking that they would provide technical help, and would not give Tshombe refuge.

What shook him was that he was told bluntly that there were two courses open to him. It was either joint action under UN, or to go it alone. If he chose the latter he could not expect support from Africa. He would have, indeed, to go it alone.

Lumumba decided to go it alone, and chose the lonely road. Within a month two cherished idols lay shattered on the ground. His illusions vanished. He could not have faith in the UN any more and if this was Pan–Africanism, then it was better to do without it. The bitterness and the grim awakening to the new realities would have made many a man hoist the flag of surrender and sue for peace, and repent before his former colonial masters. Not so Lumumba. He braced himself to fight. A friend who was with him during this crucial period said: 'Lumumba was kept going by his fantastic energy and ability to work and the rightness of the cause he represented, and he often said, "The Congo made me, and I shall make the Congo".'

There was, however, a glimmer of light for Lumumba when Sékou Touré and Nkrumah made it clear that they intended to withdraw their forces under the UN and to place them directly under the command of Lumumba. Imperialism was shocked. Hammarskjold was reported to have been very distressed. That could be understood, for if this could snowball and if other countries did the same, then the Congo operation would completely get out of their hands, and the troops would turn out to be real liberators. There was a great deal of flurry and more trafficking at diplomatic tables. Finally, the UN produced another resolution on the Congo, not substantially different from the first one.

Imperialism viewed with some hesitation and even trepidation the possible outcome of the Leopoldville Conference. They did not know just what Free Africa would do in a crisis where a choice had to be made. The Leopoldville Conference might have swung the way of Ghana and Guinea. But the results were beyond their wildest expectations. They could not have expected a better performance had they themselves called it. In endorsing the actions of the UN the Conference in fact passed a vote of 'no confidence' in Lumumba. The umbrella of protection which imperialism feared Africa might give Lumumba did not materialize.

Their agents then unsheathed their swords, sharpened their axes, loaded their rifles and like a pack moved in on Lumumba. In a sense, the Leopoldville Conference sealed the fate of Lumumba, for it gave the puppets the green light to go ahead.

18

THE KASAVUBU AND MOBUTU COUPS

THE orders went out that Lumumba should be eliminated. However, he should be eased out by constitutional means as far as possible. Since Kasavubu was the President, he was thus pushed on to the stage. The African delegates from the Leopoldville Conference had scarcely reported to their Heads of State when Kasavubu announced that he had decided to dismiss Lumumba and to dissolve parliament. In a radio broadcast on 5 September 1960, he said: 'I have most important news to announce. The Prime Minister who was named by the King of Belgium has betrayed the mission assigned to him. He has been governing arbitrarily and even now he is in the midst of throwing his country into a civil war. That is why I have decided immediately to dissolve parliament.' He declared that a new government under Joseph Ileo, President of the Senate, was to be set up.

This outrageous statement could well have come from any Belgian minister but it was the voice of Kasavubu who uttered these disgusting words. If there was one truly representative government that the Congo has had in its tragic history it was the one headed by Lumumba. For the sake of national unity he allowed past and bitter quarrels to be forgotten and he included in his government all the parties which were represented in parliament except Kalondji's breakaway group. Even CONAKAT was represented. Ileo came from Kasai and thus this province had representation, even if the Kalondji's supporters were not in. How then could Kasavubu call this arbitrary rule? Further, the civil war was brought in by Belgian aggression, and Kasavubu knew very well how he as President was not allowed to land in Katanga. But then this was the voice of the colonial masters coming out through Kasavubu.

Lumumba replied with characteristic speed and vigour the very same evening. He said: 'The popular government will remain in power. I proclaim that as from today, Kasavubu who has betrayed the nation by collaborating with the Belgians and the Flemish, is no longer the Head of State.'

The Prime Minister was ready to do battle with his President who had joined the traitors. He had to contend with two occupying powers. He was faced with rebellions in Kasai fomented by Forminière, and using Kalondji, as well as secessionist moves in Lower Congo. But these were enemies who were open, and Lumumba welcomed this, for he knew who they were and how to fight them.

However, it was the fifth column within his own government which worried him, for he did not see clearly who they were, and could not gauge their strength. The crisis now forced them to come out in the open. One such hidden enemy was Justin Bomboko, his Foreign Minister who had in fact chaired the Leopoldville Pan-African Conference. Kasavubu to put the stamp of legality to his coup had obtained the signatures of two cabinet ministers. One of them was Bomboko.

Kasavubu in his haste had made a tactical blunder. He had by-passed parliament, both the Chamber and the Senate, the highest organs of the State, which were elected by the people. In a counter attack, therefore, Lumumba called both Houses together on the 7 September. In the Chamber 90 out of 137 members were present. Only the openly fascist members of CONAKAT and the KALONDJIS stayed away. Kasavubu's own party was present. Thus it had equal opportunity to present its views to Parliament. Lumumba threw down the gauntlet and turned the Assembly into a court to judge both their actions. The tactics employed by Lumumba were brilliant. He spoke for two hours, and he was deliberately conciliatory. Kasavubu's supporters were put on the defensive. The Chamber passed a resolution declaring both the actions of Lumumba and Kasavubu as invalid. The voting was 60 in favour and 19 against, and there were two abstentions. Lumumba voted with the majority. Lumumba thus won the first round clearly and without any doubt.

In the second round, he faced the traitors Bomboko and Ileo. Bomboko had to explain his treachery before the Senate. Lumumba went on the attack and did not spare his punches, and hit not only at the rank betrayal of Kasavubu, but exposed mercilessly the role of the two occupying forces, the insidious role of the UN and the open enemies, the Belgian aggressors. Lumumba carried the House. The resolution went beyond his expectations. The Kasavubu coup was condemned by the Senate by 41 votes to 2, with 6 abstentions.

When Kasavubu had dismissed Lumumba the idea was to form a government with Ileo at the head. It was to be a broadly based government to include all except the 'extremists'. But now with the adverse vote by Parliament itself, this looked ridiculous and foolish. It was clear that they were being pushed on the stage by outsiders.

Lumumba did not rest on his laurels after this victory. He called a joint sitting of both the Chamber and the Senate. The plotters were thoroughly discredited and were demoralized. The joint sitting gave Lumumba full powers to deal with the situation as it arose, although a parliamentary delegation was appointed to supervise these powers. Out of 116 members present, 88 gave him these powers. So much then for puppet Kasavubu's assertion that Lumumba was governing arbitrarily.

When Kasavubu announced his coup, the Belgians in Leopoldville toasted the news with drinks. They urged Tshombe to join hands with him. Belgian Ministers in Brussels were delighted and promised him full support. The US officials while making no public comment said privately: 'It is about time.' Within a week Lumumba had broken this network of conspiracy and had seized the initiative once again.

Lumumba's victory was a blow to the US dominated UN command, for in the crisis it had openly sided with Kasavubu. A correspondent of *Christian Science Monitor* wrote on the 7 September 1960 that: 'What the UN is in fact doing, observers here say is that it is helping to oust Patrice Lumumba from the premiership of the Congo.' The reporter of *Le Belge Libre* was equally forthright when he wrote: 'If Messrs Kasavubu and Ileo finally win the victory they deserve, they will owe it to the United Nations. Without UN authority, Lumumba would in a few hours regain control with the few hundreds of those loyal to him.'

Bourgeois institutions are meant to be instruments to carry out the policies of the dominant class, the bourgeoisie. Once again Lumumba seizing the initiative, and not giving his enemies time to regroup and corrupt, turned the tables on the agents of imperialism by using their own parliamentary institution against them. The bourgeoisie in their deception of the people, spread the fairy tale that all power emanates from parliament, the highest legislative organ of the land. Yet it was parliament that passed a vote of no confidence in Kasavubu and gave Lumumba full emergency powers.

The victory in parliament was but a reflection of what was taking place amongst the people, who were moving towards their premier. When the coup of Kasavubu took place ABAKO intellectuals for the first time refused to support their own leader. This showed that they were no longer pre-

156

pared to say, 'My tribe right or wrong'. They were beginning to judge political issues from a political standpoint.

However, of particular significance to Africa, was that in this so-called 'constitutional crisis', Lumumba was able to uncover and expose the fifth column in the Congo; that is, he was able to expose the leaders of parties, heads of governments, heads of ministries and top civil servants, who were prepared to sell their country and the independence of the people, to foreigners. He exposed the role of the bourgeoisie, which was prepared to join hands with their former colonial masters or other imperialist powers, and to push their own country into the position of a semi-colony.

The Congo was ahead of Africa in one respect. The class struggle had broken out with all intensity and ferocity, a struggle which the rest of the continent was to experience later. In this struggle in the Congo, realignment and polarization rapidly took place. Imperialism, through the UN, and the Belgian aggressors, with puppets like Kasavubu, Tshombe and Ileo representing the bourgeoisie, stood on the one hand, and on the other the mass of the workers, peasants and intellectuals who had cast their lot with the people. In this latest phase of struggle, Lumumba did not ask for battle, but once it was thrust on him, he fought like a tiger.

Imperialism realized that in Lumumba it was dealing with a tough and experienced foe. As Kasavubu's fifth column was in complete disarray, imperialism rushed in reinforcements, and put on the stage another column, this time a real army, led by Mobutu. The 13 September was a day for victory for Lumumba and his forces for it was then that the joint session of both Houses gave him emergency powers. The very next day Mobutu announced that the Armée Nationale Congolaise (ANC) had seized power.

Mobutu's announcement that he was taking over in order to get the country out of difficulties was made over the radio. In his broadcast he stated that the army intended to neutralize the Head of State, the 'two rival' governments and parliament until 31 December 1960. The government of the people was to be replaced by a 'College des Universitaires' (College of University Students).

157

Kasavubu's initial reaction to Mobutu's action was that he 'was insolent'. Actually, to the majority of the people as well as to outsiders, there could be no other view for Mobutu was in the political sense a nobody. He had no standing in parliament and if he joined the cabinet it was as an appointee of Lumumba. From 1958 Mobutu was a member of the MNC and he soon wormed his way into Lumumba's confidence as one who was bright and politically honest.

Lumumba's initial reaction to Mobutu's coup was favourable although he might have seen the red light in Mobutu's refusal to come to Lumumba's aid when his Prime Minister and his party leader asked him to restrain Kasavubu. But Lumumba made a mistake. He recognized his opponents and enemies, but did not always assess his friends correctly. His deep trust in them sometimes precluded his better judgement. The Mobutu who announced his coup was a new Mobutu. The CIA had understood him and made for the weak point in his armour, his overweening and inordinate ambition. It was not enough to be Chief of Staff; he could well be the Head of State. By 14 September 1960 he had already gone too far, for he had 'withdrawn from politics to concentrate on his new position as Chief of Staff'. In other words, he could not turn his back on his masters. Tulley, in his book: *The CIA: the Inside Story* wrote that Mobutu was on its payroll and was regarded as one of its 'bright' discoveries. And the CIA was pleased because who could be in a better position to destroy Lumumba than one who was right in the office of Lumumba and knew all the secrets of the organization, as well as the key members? The CIA did not even bother to hide their man. While Lumumba was battling with Kasavubu and Ileo in parliament, the CIA, through the UN officials was organizing an impressive ceremony of pay parades in which Mobutu was to be given the credit for paying the soldiers. The UN records show that 5 million Congolese francs were paid to the soldiers in Leopoldville. If there was another instance of the flagrant breach of instructions by ONUC force it was this. It was additional proof that the UN was going over and above the legally elected government of the country with the sole purpose of undermining it. It showed how low the US were prepared to stoop. Where has one heard of a foreign power giving money to an official of the army over and above the legal government? This would amount to treason, and its perpetrators would be liable to execution. But the CIA believed that it was a law unto itself. If it could manipulate the United Nations, then who was Lumumba? Impartial observers noted that, 'by all accounts Mobutu had a considerable amount of money at his disposal. In this way he was able to win the allegiance of the garrisons'.

If Mobutu's action took Lumumba by surprise it was not so with the diplomats of the West. Colonel Sinclair, the military attaché at the British embassy, who had contacts with Mobutu, says that he knew several days in advance that a coup was in the offing. The ONUC officials could not hide their satisfaction and even claimed credit, for it was the payment of the troops by them that bolstered Mobutu's authority over the Leopoldville garrisons.

Just who was in real control of the situation may be judged by who benefited by the two subsequent actions of Mobutu. On 17 September, he closed down the Soviet and Czech embassies. The Chinese did not have an embassy, or otherwise he would have closed that down as well. A month later, the Ghanaian embassy met the same fate, and the Ghanaian ambassador to the Congo, Andrew Djin, and Nathaniel Welbeck, a Minister in Nkrumah's Government, had to leave the country.

It was odd that an African country should expel Africans and allow foreigners like the Americans and British to operate freely. But then it showed the orientation of Mobutu's régime. Secondly, members of the College of Commissioners, supposed to be 'technicians', had one qualification in common. They were hardened anti-Lumumbists, for its President, Bomboko, and several commissioners, the most important being Mbeka, Ndele, Kazadi, and Nussbaumer, had been recruited from among Lumumba's relentless opponents. Another qualification that these 'experts' had was that they were in contact with former lecturers and teachers, and the result was that the Belgians soon moved right back into the government machinery. It was Africanization in reverse.

Mobutu's coup was from the Right, and dangerous, for it was carried out through the State's instrument of coercion, the army, and backed by an unlimited flow of US dollars.

Kwame Nkrumah in his *Class Struggle in Africa* says that military coup d'états are forms of struggle, the object being the seizure of political power. Though carried out by the special organ or the State apparatus, seemingly isolated from society, they reflect class interests. He shows that within six years, from January 1963 to December 1969, there were 25 coups in Africa, involving diverse States from Togo, Gabon, Dahomey, to Sierra Leone, Mali and Ghana. He further adds, that behind every coup, 'there are the neo-colonialist powers teleguiding and supporting the neocolonialist State and power struggles within the reactionary bourgeois power élites; and on the other hand, there are the awakening African masses revealing the growing strength of the African socialist revolution. The African masses, when political independence was achieved, did not for a time discern the hidden hand of neocolonialism concealed behind the newly independent government.'[48]

If Sudan is omitted, then the first military coup which started a chain reaction, and which has still to run its course, took place in the Congo. A feature of the Congo situation was that foreign intervention was unconcealed. The Belgians invaded openly, using Tshombe and Kalondji as shields. US imperialism, through the UN, acted openly. First there was a plot to oust Lumumba through constitutional means and to instal a civilian government, and when that misfired, Mobutu's army was brought into the front line. So clever was the manipulation that one puppet did not know what the other was plotting. Yet the threads that bound them tied them to the one master.

It has been emphasized again that one of the features of the national liberation movement was its lack of ideological content. However, nowhere has its lack of understanding proved to be so disastrous as its failure to grasp the role of the military. Leaders, with the notable exceptions of

Nkrumah and Sékou Touré who always emphasized the sham nature of political autonomy without economic independence, believed that once they had political power they had real power. They believed that the fundamental function was to silence and isolate the political opposition and win over a majority in parliament to ensure absolute supremacy. These were the rules of the game they knew, for that is what they had been taught. This is what they saw in the Western countries, that when a government lost a parliamentary majority it resigned like a 'gentleman'. This is how it believed that imperialism would behave in Africa; that it would have no truck with an unconstitutional government. The leaders ignored the soldier in the barracks, for because he did not take part in party political fights, they believed that he had no politics. That was the mistake. The soldier had his politics. It was the politics of his superiors and it was the army that the departing colonial powers held on to, to the very last. Top European officers retained command of strategic military sectors till the very end. Even when the posts were Africanized the top posts went to those soldiers who had received their training in Sandhurst or St Cyr or other Western military academies. It was through the army and the civil service that imperialism still retained control, even while it granted independence.

It was after wave upon wave of military coups that the nationalist leaders, embarking along the road of national reconstruction, realized that it was not enough to replace Europeans with Africans at the top only, but that the army should be thoroughly politicized. The army had always had its politics, which was usually that of the ruling class, but now an attempt was made to integrate the army with the people so that it could be transformed into a peoples' army. However, a further growth in the consciousness of the people has resulted in the decision to arm the people through the peoples' militia.

Lumumba, like other Heads of State, took charge of Defence. But not being a soldier the real power lay in the hand of the Commander or the Chief of Staff. He had not given much thought to the role of the military as a factor in society until the end when the Stanleyville Government took power. His models were some of the African countries. He too retained Janssens, a Belgian, as top military commander after independence. It was only after the revolt of the Force Publique that he realized what resentment there was against the Belgian military, and thus he dismissed him. It was then that he appointed Lundula as Commander, and Mobutu as Chief of Staff.

Lumumba had not the time to keep vigilance on these top army men. The CIA went straight for Mobutu and other officers, and bribed and corrupted them so that they became Judases. Mobutu's neutrality over the Lumumba and Kasavubu crisis stemmed from the fact that he had already made up his mind who was to be his future master. It was to be neither Lumumba nor Kasavubu, but the USA.

Over a half a million people had voted for Lumumba in the elections. Since he became premier rapid strides had been made amongst the people. Lumumba carried parliament with him when challenged by Ileo and Kasavubu. Now with the Mobutu coup, what was being tested was what was to be the fighting capacity of those who backed Lumumba electorally. Imperialism had learnt that it was enough to have just a few hundred soldiers, and to distribute them in certain parts of the capital, to surround and take over certain strategic places and then the government can be overthrown.

The military played an insignificant part in the struggle for independence. Who has ever heard of any of the present military leaders having been thrown in jail by any of the colonial governments? They were insignificant, and not known to the people. And if they were known, they were hated, for they had been used by the colonial masters to brow-beat the population, shoot down strikers, hound peasant guerrillas and to break up peoples' demonstrations. In the post independence era, whenever imperialism saw that it was losing its grip it pushed the military into the front line. In this however it showed its desperation, for the army is imperialism's last line of defence.

19

LUMUMBA AND NKRUMAH

WHEN Lumumba was battling against elements of the fifth column which had reared their heads with the Kasavubu coup, behind Lumumba's back and against his wishes, UN troops moved in and closed the radio and the airport. The soldiers who carried out these orders were Ghanaians. Lumumba took some of his loyal troops to reopen the radio, but he was refused entry. It was a bitter blow for Lumumba to see Ghanaian troops preventing him from broadcasting to his own people during such a crisis. The imperialist world could not help but be happy, for here were African troops tying the hands of Lumumba as a step to help in his overthrow. Meanwhile, the UN allowed Tshombe to broadcast freely on Radio Elizabethville; and Kasavubu was using Brazzaville radio to whip up anti-Lumumbist feeling.

Lumumba sent the following message to Nkrumah: 'I hasten to express to you my indignation regarding the aggressive and hostile attitude of Ghanaian soldiers towards me and my Government. ... At 4.30 p.m. today, 11 September, accompanied by my soldiers, I personally went to take over the radio station. The Ghana troops, however, opposed my decision with hostility and went to the extent of seizing arms from my soldiers. The Ghana soldiers even wanted to shoot me and my soldiers.

'To these incidents add also the hostile declaration of General Alexander of your army against the Government of the Republic. All these acts committed by your soldiers are far from proving the friendship I wanted to maintain with you and your people. In the circumstances, I feel obliged to renounce the help of your troops in view of the fact that they are in a state of war against our Republic. Instead of helping us in our difficulties, your soldiers are openly siding with the enemy to fight us. With my profound regret, I am your good friend.'

Nkrumah not only understood, but felt very deeply what the denial of the use of the radio meant to Lumumba. In a letter to Hammarskjold he said: 'Radio Brazzaville which is controlled by France, a permanent member of the Security Council, is allowed to indulge in the most violent propaganda against the legitimate Lumumba Government. Radio Elizabethville, which is in effect under Belgian control, is also allowed to indulge in similar propaganda. Thus Ghana is used virtually to tie Lumumba's hands behind him while a permanent member of the Security Council is allowed to whip him.'[49]

In a reply to Lumumba, Nkrumah showed how extremely distressed he was over the whole situation for: 'I also find myself in an embarrassing and invidious position in respect of the way in which my Ghana troops are being used in the Congo, though I have been fighting like mad day and night on your behalf. . . . If Ghana troops are to placed completely at your disposal, then you and your Government must find some way to declare that in this struggle, Ghana and the Congo are one. Only thus would it be possible for my Ghana troops to operate legitimately with the Congolese forces.'[50]

The essence of Lumumbaism was a united Congo, free from tribalism, and internal economic reform based on the elimination of the exploitation of man by man. Externally, it stood for Pan–Africanism, and a policy of non-alignment.

Pan–Africanism was not just an idea for both Nkrumah and Lumumba to be discussed at certain meetings. Both realized that continental unity was the only way to fight imperialism. So close and complete was the agreement between the two on this fundamental issue that they entered into an Agreement.[51] For tactical reasons it was kept a secret at the time it was signed. Nkrumah writing seven years later however, saw fit to release the text of it. It was on the pattern of the Ghana–Guinea–Mali union, and was worded as follows:

Secret Agreement signed by Osagyefo, Dr Kwame Nkrumah and His Excellency Mr Patrice Lumumba,

Prime Minister of the Republic of the Congo, at Accra on
8 August 1960.

The President of the Republic of Ghana and the Prime
Minister of the Republic of the Congo have given serious
thought to the idea of African unity and have decided to
establish with the approval of the Government and
peoples of their respective States, among themselves a
UNION OF AFRICAN STATES. The Union
would have a Republican Constitution within a federal
framework.

The Federal Government would be responsible for:

(a) Foreign Affairs;
(b) Defence;
(c) The issue of a Common Currency;
(d) Economic Planning and Development.

There would be no customs barriers between any parts of
the Federation. There would be a Federal Parliament and
a Federal Head of State. The Capital of the Union should
be Leopoldville. Any State or Territory in Africa is free to
join this Union. The above Union presupposes Ghana's
abandonment of the Commonwealth.

Dated at Accra this 8th day of August 1960

KWAME NKRUMAH   PATRICE LUMUMBA

President of the   Prime Minister
Republic of Ghana   of the Congo

This historic and far-reaching document shows the
thinking of the most politically-advanced figures produced
by the African nationalist movement. They thought of the
struggle in continental terms, and had seen through the limited goal of control of a piece of territory where one could be
President or Prime Minister. It shows too the close identity
of views on these basic issues. How is it then that a month
later, Lumumba was to write to his political inspirer and his
mentor, of the hostility of Ghana's soldiers, and to ask for
their withdrawal? The Ghanaian troops were carrying out
the orders of the UN, and *not* the orders of President

Nkrumah. Djin, a great admirer of Lumumba, and Ghana's ambassador to the Congo represented Nkrumah, while the commanders of the Ghanaian troops in the Congo, Alexander, Ankrah and Otu, represented imperialism and stabbed both Nkrumah and Lumumba in the back. This dichotomy was not confined to Ghana, but also to Guinea, Tanzania and other radical States. If Nkrumah, Sékou Touré, Nyerere and Lumumba represented the interests of the workers and peasants and the national interests, then the Busias, Ankrahs, Fodeba Keitas, Kambonas, the Tshombes and Kasavubus represented imperialism. The struggle between the two was in the arena of the control of the State machinery.

Imperialism knew very well the close bond of comradeship which existed between Lumumba and Nkrumah. Throughout the Congo crisis, Nkrumah was in close touch with the Congolese premier, advising, counselling, and also warning him. Thus in a letter dated 22 August 1960, Nkrumah telling Lumumba not to despair wrote: 'The problem seems to me to be to convert the Congolese national army into an efficient fighting force within a very short space of time. You must adopt Tactical Action. Remember, the forces pitched against you are legion. But the odds are in your favour and you will succeed if only you handle the situation carefully and tactfully.'[52]

Among the forces pitched against Lumumba were certain Ghanaian officers and bureaucrats committed to imperialism. The Ghanaian military, under the orders of the UN, harassed Lumumba, disarmed his troops, and blocked the movement of his supporters and government officials. The Ghanaian supporters of imperialism struck at Lumumba, in 1960. Six years later these Ghanaians also struck at Kwame Nkrumah. The Ghanaians of imperialism did not see fellow-Africans or fellow-Ghanaians. They saw their class enemies in Lumumba and Nkrumah, who represented the workers and peasants.

The flouting of law and order, constitution, parliament, the recourse to violence and murder, showed that the class struggle had erupted side by side with the national struggle. Just as Nkrumah, Sékou Touré, and Modeba Keita had to forge alliances, so too did the bourgeoisie of Africa. Albert Youlou of Congo Brazzaville, Kasavubu, Ankrah, Otu and others like them, had already sought out their friends and taken up positions against those they regarded as their class enemies.

Lumumba was arrested on 12 September 1960, and Djin wrote to Nkrumah: 'Without losing a moment I commanded a part of my personal guard, seven in number, to proceed with me at once to the place of his arrest. ... At the Camp Headquarters I discussed with Brigadier Otu and Colonel Ankrah my plans for releasing Mr Lumumba. The two Commanders considered my plans inadvisable and stated that they could not lend hand to me in such an action until they had been released from UNO Command. ... I would also like to add that I regretted the attitude adopted by our Commanders and their continued lack of cooperation. If the Army had seen my political point of view which I had on many occasions attempted to explain to them and had supported my plan they would completely have retrieved by their gallant action all that Ghana had lost in the Congo and would have shown to UNO and all and sundry that Ghana and its President were firmly behind Lumumba and his Government. ... I was particularly anxious that UNO who had all along played the political game against Lumumba to know that Ghana stood firmly behind Lumumba, but once more our soldiers proved uncooperative and unreliable at the critical moment.'[53] It was clear that the representatives of the Ghanaian bourgeoisie, in alliance with imperialism, were determined to see that Lumumba, the representative of the workers and peasants, did not succeed.

Behind the confusion and chaos one thing was clear, that an alliance was being formed between imperialism and certain layers of the bourgeoisie, on a continental scale, under the banner of UN operations in the Congo. Ankrah and Otu knew very well how the Ghanaian people and their President felt about the treatment meted out to Lumumba, and therefore his release would win their approval. But they chose their new masters who paid them well publicly, and probably paid them also huge sums privately.

In another sense, imperialism was also testing African army officers to see if they would serve their countries or imperialism. They revealed their choice by their actions in the Congo. They proved 'uncooperative and unreliable in the Congo', and they also proved to be treacherous in Ghana six years later. It was no accident that Ankrah was chosen to lead the counter-revolutionary National Liberation Council (NLC), after the overthrow of Kwame Nkrumah on 24 February 1966. In the eyes of imperialism, he had earned his promotion by his actions in the Congo. An officer who could defy and turn against a Prime Minister of a sister African country could well be relied on to turn against his own President.

In the nationalist phase of the struggle, imperialism and its columns were seen in the person of the white man who was the administrator, the priest, or the business man. Africa had still to realize that the 'enemy within' was really within, in the top layers of the bureaucracy. Only a decade later, as a result of a further growth of political consciousness African revolutionaries have come to understand that African society, like its Asian and European counterparts, has classes, and that the class struggle was breaking out. It is this that brought about a polarization to create the two Ghanas, two Tanzanias, two Congos and two Guineas. The struggle of Nkrumah, Sékou Touré, Nyerere and Lumumba against Busia, Fodeba Keita, Kambona, Tshombe and others like them, was but a manifestation of class struggle. One of the first shots were fired in the Congo, and claimed Lumumba as the first victim.

One of the favourite tricks of imperialism and its ideologists is to create division amongst revolutionary comrades. The literary hacks are called upon to bring out their poisonous pens and to perform the dirty and messy jobs. In the Congo an attempt was made to drive a wedge between Lumumba and Nkrumah. We give one such specimen, a passage written by Colin Legum in his foreword to *Congo, My Country*: 'Lumumba's behaviour drove the UN representatives and his friends to despair. Although he had originally made President Kwame Nkrumah, his closest political confidant, he began to ignore him once Dr Nkrumah's advice began to conflict with his own increasingly unrealistic ideas.'[54]

The very opposite was the case, for it was at this very time of crisis that bonds were strengthened. Misunderstanding on the behaviour of Ghanaian troops arose, but this was cleared up. The comradeship that developed between Lumumba and Nkrumah was rare indeed and it was able to survive the sternest of tests. At the time of the treacherous action of Alexander, Ankrah and Otu, in mobilizing troops against Lumumba which might have been expected to have created a chasm, Lumumba wrote a letter to Nkrumah, giving the lie to the accusation that Lumumba and Nkrumah had begun to go their separate ways. This was perhaps the last letter that Lumumba was able to write before his house arrest and subsequent flight. It was certainly the last to Nkrumah. It shows how Lumumba was prepared to work with Nkrumah on their common goal to the very end. He wrote:

> Mr President and dear Friend, it is with very real pleasure that I received your several messages, and I thank you most heartily. I have taken into consideration all the advice you have given me and have spoken about it with Mr Djin, the Ambassador.
>
> Mr Djin and the ambassadors of the United Arab Republic, Morocco and Tunisia, have proposed reconciliation between President Kasavubu and myself. ... Mr Kasavubu does not wish for any reconciliation, and prefers to play the game of the imperialists against Africa. And so, as you will see, the fault is not mine. Everything is being done to stifle the Republic of the Congo and subject it to the tutelage of the Western Powers. ... The Congo–Ghana Union will be immediately achieved and I shall submit the plan for Parliament's approval. Kasavubu was the obstacle in the way of this Union. ... Nevertheless, I should like to ask you to continue the struggle at the United Nations. You will have to send me military reinforcements at Stanleyville. Congo and Ghana must fight together until final victory is achieved. ...

The United Nations, as a result of their mischievous action in the Congo, wished to sow the seeds of discord between the Congo and Ghana. The situation has just been clarified and our ties are now stronger than ever. Consequently there is no further disagreement between us.

You can rely on me and I on you. Today we are one, and our countries are one.

PS. Parliament has given me full powers and I have the law behind me.[55]

What could be more touching than this, showing the warmth between these two leaders? For in fact it was to be Lumumba's farewell letter to Kwame Nkrumah.

20

DUAL POWER IN THE CONGO

MOBUTU was an upstart, and so was every one in the so-called Commissioners around him. Whereas a case could be made out for Kasavubu in that he had been a long time in politics, and had some support even if it was on tribal grounds, no such case could be put for Mobutu and his coterie. The hidden pillar that propped him and supplied him liberally with dollars and arms now showed its hand openly.

Hitherto, the US was careful in using the UN machinery to achieve its ends. The troops that dislodged Lumumba were under the command of the UN, although they served the US. Even when the 5 million francs of CIA money was handed to Mobutu, care was taken to see that it was through the auspices of the UN.

The arrival of Dayal as UN representative in the Congo forced the hand of the US. Dayal, from India, was no ardent follower of Lumumba, but on the other hand he would have no truck with Mobutu because as he saw it the Congolese constitution did not speak of them or their authority in any way. The constitution had no place for the military who usurped power by sheer force of arms at the bidding of a foreign power. He thus saw to it that Lumumba was not in any way molested by Mobutu's troops, or arrested by them. But the UN representative would not dislodge or disarm Mobutu's troops ringed round his house because he was bound by his mandate. In short, Lumumba was now a prisoner of both Mobutu, as well as the UN, which in fact was there to protect him.

On 2 November, Dayal submitted his report to the UN. He singled out the Belgian advisers in Leopoldville and Katanga, and accused them of being behind the troubles in the Congo. He also condemned the military coup of Mobutu and asked that this be ended as speedily as possible. In pleading for a return of the constitutional government he said that in the confused political situation which prevailed, the only two institutions whose foundations still stood were the Office of the Chief of State and Parliament. If the minimum conditions of non-interference and security could be established, it would open the way to the leaders of the country to seek a peaceful solution through the medium of these two institutions. This information was released as an official UN report. Its message was clear, and read correctly, by both friends and enemies of Lumumba. It meant that he could return to power.

This forced the hands of the US, for its spokesman said that it would only accept the return of parliamentary government if the nominee of President Kasavubu was made premier, that is, under the leadership of Joseph Ileo and not Patrice Lumumba. Openly now backing Belgium in its role of aggression and disregarding the very Security Council Resolution to which it was a party condemning Belgium, the US now made it clear that it had every confidence in the good faith of Belgium in its declared desire to be of assistance to the Congo; and that the US was therefore unable to accept the implications to the contrary contained in the various parts of Dayal's Report.

The issue of who should be premier had already been decided by the people of the Congo when they gave the MNC a landslide victory. It was also further confirmed when the Belgian minister could not find a formateur to form a government other than Lumumba. Again then, the Parliament of the Congo decided that Lumumba should be the premier. If there was to be further evidence, there was the joint sitting of both Chambers of Parliament that gave Lumumba overwhelming support as against Ileo and other candidates. Here then was the US blatantly interfering in the internal affairs of a country by saying that it, as a super power bullying and dictating to a small country, should say who should be its premier, and who should not.

Why the US behaved so arrogantly was indicated by an American correspondent: 'Never before on the Congo issue, and rarely before in Hammarskjold's tenure of office, has the US publicly disagreed with the Secretary-General or disputed his judgement on a major issue. Clearly, observers say, the stakes must have been regarded as huge in Washington.'

From then onwards, the US worked feverishly and relentlessly to oust Lumumba throwing all caution to the winds. This it did through the UN machinery, when the UN Assembly decided to seat the Kasavubu delegation, and not the delegation sent by Lumumba. The result of the vote was 53 for, 24 against and 19 abstentions. The *Le Monde* correspondent expressed the view of many when he said that the vote was a victory for the American 'big stick'. The *Observer* correspondent held the same view when he said: 'The Kasavubu vote was obtained by intense US and Western lobbying behind the scenes at the UN, and by the decision of the African States of the French Community to vote for Kasavubu'.

The African States of the French Community consisted then of 11 States. These were Senegal, Ivory Coast, Upper Volta, Niger, Dahomey, Cameroon, Gabon, Chad, Central African Republic, Congo Brazzaville and Madagascar. Just why they voted against Lumumba could be revealed in a speech by the Abbe Fulbert Youlou, an out and out slave of French imperialism and a close adviser of Mobutu. In the Assembly he said. 'The situation in the Congo was worse in

November than it was in July, and this was because the United Nations was preventing a constitutionally established political leader (Kasavubu) from legally arresting a rebel and a malefactor.' This servant had however forgotten conveniently that parliament, and particularly the Senate, had in fact rejected Kasavubu's actions. It was the President then, that should have resigned as a result of the vote of no confidence in him.

Other African states which made possible the seating of the Kasavubu delegation by their abstentions were Ethiopia, Libya, Sudan, Tunisia and Upper Volta. Nigeria did not participate in the voting.

The lining up of certain African States to vote for the US-backed resolutions, or to abstain in order not to offend the US, struck at the very concept of African unity and independence. Had the US sponsored a contrary resolution then these would have voted accordingly. The UN Assembly vote meant that the US and the other Western imperialist powers could seat or unseat the delegation of any government, even if it was completely against the wishes of the people, by seating a delegation of its own choice. But this goes directly against the very parliamentary system to which Western ideologists pay so much lip service. And this was the point that the delegate from Togo made when he said: 'We are not fighting for the person of Lumumba, but the principle of legality and parliamentary government, a principle which was clearly violated by the vote of the General Assembly. Even if Lumumba disappears tomorrow, the elements which he represents will not disappear.'

Therefore, what the traitorous clique represented by the Kasavubu-Ileo faction failed to achieve in their own Parliament, they had to achieve through foreign intervention by US manipulation of the UN. The masters had to come out openly to their rescue. But the US itself could not have succeeded were it not for the support of the puppet African governments. While Africa was being granted freedom and independence, the puppet States were already lending a hand in Africa's reconquest. If African unity is to have any real meaning, then what has to be clarified is unity for what?

With and against whom? On the Congo issue, the majority of the African States united with the US and Belgium, their imperialist masters, to oust a legally elected prime minister and the government of Patrice Lumumba, and to install a puppet government which, admitted by all, had no national or popular support.

Lumumba's electoral victory, which would have enabled him to establish a national government, was snatched away from him first by Belgian aggression, then by UN occupation, and then by US manipulation of the vote in the Assembly of the UN. These were all attempts to thwart him from carrying out the people's mandate.

Lumumba fought back with all the methods available to him and with a series of brilliant counter attacks turned the tables against his enemies. Possible defeats were turned into victories. Lumumba knew that if the arena of struggle was to be in Parliament or among the masses his enemies would have no chance. But imperialism chose the military, and Mobutu as its chief agent. It was indeed ironical that this was the very organ, the army, and the very person, Mobutu, whom Lumumba trusted to come in to help him in establishing power, which entered the arena as a counter revolutionary force.

If after July, traitors like Bomboko, Ileo, Kasavubu and Mobutu left him, other like Gizenga, the Vice-Premier, Kasamura, Piere Mulele and Antoine Gbenye drew even closer, although they did not belong to the MNC. So great was the growing solidarity between the various groups and the MNC, that Lumumba decided to merge his organization with the PSA, CEREA and elements of the BALUBA-KAT to form a new national party, with grass roots amongst the masses.

Those who gravitated towards Lumumba were the Congolese youth, and these were politically mature. The heat and fire of the struggle was such that during the years leading up to 1960, and particularly after July 1960 they became politically aware very quickly. Intelligent and quick, and not directly involved in diplomatic manoeuvres, they understood, as did Lumumba, that the only language the enemies would understand would be that of force. It was the counter revolutionary force that dislodged Lumumba; then only revolutionary force could put him and his government back in power. This meant that not only the people would have to be politicized, but they should also be armed. Against a puppet army, they decided to create an army that belonged to, and was loyal to, the people. This meant only one thing, to take the road to Stanleyville, their base area.

Lumumba and his fellow nationalist revolutionaries had travelled full circle. They were wiser for their experiences learned through the hard school of life. Belgium had given them independence with one hand and taken it away with the other through Tshombe. The UN was called in to liberate, but remained to occupy. The African States were called in to help, and they ended up chastizing their hosts. Attempts at reconciliation with Kasavubu had proved Lumumba correct, for Kasavubu had chosen his imperialist masters.

In the letter of September 1960 to Nkrumah, Lumumba had indicated that Parliament had taken a decision to remove the capital of the Congo to Stanleyville. He wrote: 'The whole country is behind the Government. The removal of the seat of the Government to Stanleyville will soon frustrate the imperialist plots, because it will be seen at once that Kasavubu is isolated and that the country is not in agreement with him.'[56]

If counter revolutionaries learn from their mistakes, so do revolutionaries. The latter understood that the only force to counter Belgian aggression and UN occupation would be the people. It would not be debates even in parliament on the legality or otherwise of this or that man's actions, it would not be the discussions at world assemblies that would be the decisive factor. It would be force, organized force of the poeple confronting and challenging the force of imperialism that would be decisive. And it was in this new confrontation, where the armed forces of revolution met the armed forces of counter revolution that it was proved once again that the country and its people were behind Lumumba.

While Lumumba was surrounded by a ring of troops, and his every movement watched, other leaders slipped away from Leopoldville and took the road to Stanleyville. From the other provincial capitals it was the same. Militants and radicals all converged towards the capital of Orientale province. And nothing could show more the degree of political consciousness of the people than that, although belonging to different tribes, they were all well received in Stanleyville. In them was the future nation. At the end of November, those who had arrived were Antoine Gizenga, Christopher Gbenye, Marcel Bisukiro, Mulele and Massena. Thomas Kanza and Andre Mandi, two highly educated Congolese who had refused to serve the College of Commissioners had also indicated their support for Lumumba. Two highly placed and popular leaders of the BALUBAKAT, Remy Mwamba and Ilunga also arrived. Last but not least came Victor Lundula, Commander of the Congolese army, who at the time of crisis remained loyal to Lumumba, and whom the imperialists could not corrupt. Kasavubu had decided to 'sack' him.

A central government was set up in Stanleyville with ministers who held similar posts in Leopoldville. But it was only after 15 December, that is, after the announcement of the arrest of Lumumba, that it openly announced itself and began to function as such.

One of the first jobs which Lundula undertook after his arrival in October, was to reorganize the army. All the officers suspected of being in the pay of imperialism and Mobutu were dismissed, dispersed, and their units were broken up. Meanwhile, there was a massive recruitment campaign to enrol new and younger people. Within a short time the provincial army had over 5,000 men. The UN troops were not only outnumbered, but also rendered powerless, for now not only had they to contend with armed force, but with soldiers who were organically linked up with the aspirations of the people.

Both Chambers of Parliament had given Lumumba full power to reorganize the government. Within a short space of two months, there arose in Stanleyville not only a government representative of the people, but an army that would now be in a position to enforce laws and decrees, and to protect its civilian leaders.

Western writers who could hardly be accused of being Lumumbists surveying this scene recognized the reality of the new force emerging round the Stanleyville Government. One of them commented: 'Within the Congo itself, the Stanleyville régime, despite its recent formation and lack of organization could certainly count on wider support than either the régime in Leopoldville or Katanga. It controlled virtually the whole of the Orientale province and enjoyed considerable support of wide areas of Kivu, Kasai, North Katanga and the western part of Leopoldville province. It carried the prestige of Lumumba's name.'[57]

The Stanleyville Government at once set about challenging the other bases of power, in Elizabethville and Leopoldville. Freed from the deadening effects of sterile debates with resolutions and amendments and counter amendments, free from conciliation attempts which the other side was not prepared to honour, the revolutionary youth of the Congo now set about organizing the population with the same fervour and determination that characterized the elections. Only now they had become wiser as a result of the knocks they had received. The youth of the Congo showed the whole of Africa what they could do. With Orientale province as the base area, they moved in all directions to establish peoples' power in other areas of the Congo.

In the process, they also showed that the UN police force was just another paper tiger. They just by-passed the UN troops stationed there, took over control, and presented a *fait accompli*. In fact, it also showed that the lower layers of the UN troops were sympathetic to the cause of the legitimate government of the Congo.

In two quick decisive moves, the army from Stanleyville, in fact a people's liberation army, because its task was to liberate the Congo from foreign domination, took over Kivu province and Northern Katanga. In the case of the latter, about 500 soldiers from Stanleyville moved secretly on 7 January 1961 into Kivu province and entered Monono in northern Katanga. The majority of the soldiers were Baluba and therefore belonged to the population. Mwamba Ilunga was with the army and it was accepted by the population. The political leaders from this area joined the liberation forces in the take-over. As a result of the support of the population, a new and separate administration was established, cutting itself off from the Tshombe Government. A new province of Lualaba was established. What was surprising was that this journey by the soldier's from Stanleyville involved travelling hundreds of miles, including a passage through Kivu. The soldiers could easily have been recognized as they belonged to a different tribe. That the move was a complete surprise meant only this, that the people supported the Balubas and their action. There were some 400 soldiers in Monono. They were taken completely by surprise, but they could do nothing about it, for not only were the liberation troops entrenched, but also they had the support of the local population. It was just as well that the UN Nigerian troops did not use force, for they would have been faced with the uprising of the entire people. However, what was more significant, was that the Belgians and the puppet Tshombe could do nothing about it, although the liberation took place right on their doorstep. Now these pompous and arrogant men showed their fear and revealed their weakness.

The people did not rest, however. They pursued their victory and attacked trains going to Katanga. The aim of this was clear. It was to bleed the Tshombe Government to the extent that it would not be able to launch a counter offensive against the base area of Stanleyville. With their outlook national now, one could see that their military strategy too oriented in this direction. The protection of their base area was more important than their own town Munono.

However, the successful thrust was only made possible as a result of an outstanding victory in Kivu province. Here, on Christmas Day in 1960, troops moved into Kivu, the capital of Kivu province, and arrested Major Singa whom they believed was in the pay of the foreigners. When President Miruho intervened to defend the Major he was also arrested. They were taken to Stanleyville. Kashamura, Minister of Information under Lumumba, took over the civil administration.

This caused panic amongst the puppets and their masters. Mobutu who was being built up as the strong man in the country, and known for his toughness, was sent to Kivu to bring these 'rebels to heel'. He used the typical tactic of deception, of announcing that he was travelling south and then heading northwards. He said he would be flying to Kasai province to prepare for Kasavubu's arrival, while in fact he had made arrangements to fly to Kivu with his forces. To effect this he had contacted the Belgians to allow him to use the airfield at Ruanda-Urundi, which adjoined Kivu province, for the landing of his troops. He wanted to take the people completely by surprise. Except for Tshombe, no other Congolese leader worthy of his name would publicly associate themselves with the former colonial masters. Therefore attack from this quarter would have been unexpected.

The invasion of Kivu was a joint enterprise with Belgium fully involved. Reports show that when Mobutu's troops landed at the airport, Belgium made available its lorries to transport troops to the Ruanda–Kivu border. In the meantime, planes had dropped hundreds of leaflets calling on the people to welcome their deliverer, Mobutu. Nigerian forces stationed there confirmed that the Belgians had assisted in the attack, and Belgian soldiers from Ruanda-Urundi were arrested in Kivu.

Mobutu had overestimated his strength, and underestimated the fierce hatred that the people had for the Belgian ex-rulers. He believed that he had just to bribe one or two army officers and one or two politicians, and that the local ANC would flock to welcome him and that the people would line up in the streets to wave at him. But nothing of the sort happened. The local ANC garrison turned against him, just as the people rose against him. The soldiers, expecting an easy victory, meeting such hostility and resistance, just panicked. The battles were very short and decisive, and Mobutu's troops fled in disorder in all directions. Some took refuge in the camp of the Nigerians, others fled to Ruanda-Urundi, but many just laid down their arms and surrendered. The attempt by counter revolution, through Mobutu, to take Kivu thus ended in disaster. The myth of Mobutu the strong man, the strategist and outstanding soldier was shattered by the unknown and unnamed soldiers and people of Kivu. The people thus collectively had demonstrated their strength once they were united.

The defeat caused not only demoralization, but also division in the camp of the puppets. Catherine Hoskyns recording this, states: 'The failure of the attempt to take over Kivu was a serious blow to the prestige of Mobutu, and to the alliance as a whole and resulted in increasing opposition to him in the army as well as among the politicians.' As a result it seems to have been fairly accepted that the army must be withdrawn from politics and that a government of politicians must replace the College of Commissioners. 'In January, Mobutu was promoted from Colonel to General ... but nothing could conceal that his authority was crumbling.'[58]

The crushing defeat of Mobutu's forces at Kivu and the successful take-over in Katanga, concrete and decisive steps in the liberation of the Congo, heartened the revolutionary forces. Their base extended now, since it rested on the armed might of the people's army from Orientale province, to Kivu and northern Katanga. The next target was the province of Equator on the border of Orientale. A pincer movement was developing to isolate Leopoldville and southern Katanga. With the establishment of dual power in the Congo, the forces of revolution based in Stanleyville were thus seizing the initiative from the forces of counter revolution, and beating them on their own plane, that of military strength. If the same momentum was kept up, then the signs were clear that a national uprising of armed people to defend their conquests was on the way.

On 10 September 1960, the Belgian Minister of Foreign Affairs said that the constitutional authorities had a duty to put Lumumba in a position where he could not cause trouble. The 'constituted authorities' had already issued a warrant for the arrest of Lumumba, and in September he was apprehended, only to be freed by the intervention of Congolese soldiers. In the crucial months of October and November, he was under house arrest with two rings of troops surrounding the building. From here he was in no position to carry out his duties as prime minister, or as leader of his party. But as Bomboko said on 4 October: 'As long as this rascal is free, there is no use working.' Even under arrest, Lumumba could demoralize his enemies.

The people of the Congo did not expect Lumumba to be overthrown in such a cynical and shameless way. They were angry that upstarts like Mobutu, and those around him in his 'College', should now take control. They were not known for any contribution they had made for the people. Their hearts went out to Lumumba particularly while he was under house arrest, and after his daring escape, and his subsequent capture and imprisonment. If there was one single factor that turned the entire Congolese people, whatever their political affiliations, against the usurpers Kasavubu and Mobutu it was just this. James O'Driscoll writing in a British newspaper observed the following: 'Support for him (Lumumba) has grown throughout the country since his capture by the forces of Colonel Mobutu. Thinking Congolese, whether his political supporters or not, feel he is, after all, the elected prime minister. Although they do not agree with his policies, they feel that he should be allowed to take office and not be thrown out at the dictates of rival political parties and the chief of the army before his Parliament has even been consulted.'[59]

This was the view of some of the educated Congolese, but the masses were even more outspoken. Kasavubu had organized a mass meeting in Luluaberg in an area believed to be his stronghold. The people however refused to listen to him and shouted back: 'Where is Lumumba? Long Live Lumumba. Uhuru.' That shook Kasavubu, for the people in the choice of slogans saw the issues clearly, that it was Lumumba and not Kasavubu, who stood for Uhuru.

The people identified Lumumba with their own aspirations. His imprisonment became their imprisonment, his pain there pain. And Mali's delegate at the UN warned the imperialists after his transfer to Leopoldville that, 'what the colonialists forget is that Lumumba is more than a man. He is a symbol. He is the incarnation of the aspirations of a whole people – of millions of Congolese and the Congolese Revolution will succeed because it is inevitable.'[60]

Lumumba outwitted his captors when he escaped from the troops of the UN and of Mobutu. He headed towards Stanleyville. But once outside the precincts of the capital, he was no longer a fugitive, but a prime minister. That is how the people saw him. At Bulungu, he stopped to buy provisions and an inhabitant recognized him. The news spread like wildfire, and at 10.30 a.m. he was practically forced to hold a public meeting before an enthusiastic crowd. He spoke of his difficulties and explained that he was going to Stanleyville not as a fugitive, but to take charge of the liberation of the national territory, in order to protect the people. It was the same at Pukulu, the enthusiastic crowd forced him to speak, and villagers poured in to hear him. At Mangai it was Pukulu all over again. But this cost him very valuable time.

What had begun as the flight of a fugitive, had in a very few days become a triumphant tour of the people's national leader and hero. And it was characteristic of Lumumba that he pushed to the background the personal danger that faced him, and pushed the cause into the forefront. He spoke not of his personal suffering at the hands of the traitors, but began rallying the people towards the new and arduous task of preparing themselves for armed struggle. This method was the only one left, to liberate the people of the Congo from Belgian aggression, and UN occupation.

The victory at Kivu and North Katanga had shown the people a way out. A bold decisive encounter with the armed might of the people achieved much more than hundreds of debates, moves and counter moves in the jungles of diplomacy. There was thus an upsurge once again all over the country.

When Lumumba was once again arrested, far from disheartening his followers, it inspired them to newer and greater efforts. Right in the very heart of reaction, followers of the MNC who had been in hiding for several months showed up openly and began to organize the masses. Other cadres went straight for the soldiers. The result was that there was a revolt of the soldiers right in the very camp in which Lumumba was imprisoned. It was then a touch-and-go affair. The rank and file soldiers had defied their officers and opened the doors of the cells where Lumumba and his colleagues had been lodged. That was on 13 January 1961. But counter-revolution read the signs of mutiny correctly. Lumumba alive, even when imprisoned, was a rally point of the Congolese people opposed to the reconquest of their country. They showed themselves boldly and fearlessly, and a national uprising meeting counter revolutionary force with revolutionary force of the people was imminent.

It was then that Kasavubu, Mobutu, and Bomboko decided to murder Lumumba. They had tried him and condemned him to death in absentia. But since they did not want the blood of Lumumba on their hands, knowing that posterity would never forgive them for the murder, they handed Lumumba and two of his close and trusted colleagues Maurice Mpolo and Joseph Okito to Tshombe for execution. The three men were removed from the military camp in Leopoldville and sent to Tshombe in Elizabethville. It was destination 'death'.

21

THE MURDER OF LUMUMBA

IN January 1960, in a speech to Amis de Présence Africaine, Lumumba related his ordeals while he was in detention under the Belgian authorities. He said: 'Everything was done to break my spirit. I was jeered at, vilified, dragged in the mud – simply because I insisted on freedom for our country.'

This was child's play to what was in store for him when he

was under the 'care and protection' of Mobutu and Kasavubu after his capture. For Lumumba had then to undergo trials and suffering that would have tested the nerves and endurance of the bravest and most courageous of men. His crazed and dehumanized captors left him with little peace as they insulted, slapped him, pulled his hair, kicked and spat on him, and broke his spectacles. Later, he was starved, and denied medical treatment. All this barbarous and outrageous treatment was designed to break his spirit and turn Lumumba, a Man, into a grovelling slave who would prostrate himself, begging for mercy. But none of this happened. Torture, both mental and physical just served to steel him further, and he maintained a dignified calm, even when obviously in pain.

Lumumba had made a daring escape from Leopoldville on the night of 27 November and had been captured on 3 December. A great deal of publicity surrounded his arrival as a captive, and under its glare a national tragedy was turned into a carnival. The question in the minds of many friends was, why did he escape and thus endanger his own life, while the UN offered him protection? But what sort of protection was this? It was the UN that had disarmed his troops; it had closed the radio station to him, and the airport, and in a hundred other ways did all to overthrow him. Having overthrown him as premier, they now protected his person. And this protection was such that he was not allowed to speak to the people, to write, or communicate. This protection was in fact castrating Lumumba, for it was destroying his political life. On this, both the UN and Mobutu were in perfect agreement, that as long as he was under house arrest he would be driven into a position where he would be impotent politically. In the meantime, reaction was being given every chance to consolidate.

The upstart commissioners who, under pressure from the Belgians, now flourished as never before were thirsting for Lumumba's blood. Only individuals like Dayal, UN representative in the Congo, showed any sympathy for Lumumba. But he was a civilian and did not control the military. His force was only a moral one. Yet he used it in his report to the Secretary General, and made a scathing attack on Mobutu and the activities of the commissioners, particularly stating that their seizure of power was blatantly illegal and unconstitutional.

Even under UN protection, Lumumba's life hung on a slender thread, for he was at its mercy. Any time for instance, Dayal could be removed, and in fact a campaign was launched that he leave the Congo. Now, with the UN Assembly voting Kasavubu in, the slender thread could snap at any moment. In any event, Lumumba had already made up his mind that occupied Congo had to be liberated. Just as he led the people to victory at the polls, he considered it his duty to lead them again in this new phase of armed struggle. He realized that the only force he could rely on was the people, and it was important that he be with them. The historic tasks which he saw ahead of him made him make up his mind. There was no alternative. Better to make a dash for it than to be a sitting duck at the mercy of his captors.

The West undoubtedly played an important part in his capture. Its press had already warned from the information of its communications network that Lumumba would attempt an escape. After the news of his departure, concealed on the floor of a car, leaked out, Mobutu made a request to a European airline company, and this supplied him not only with a machine, but also with a European pilot, who was a specialist in low altitude flying.

Another European settler contributed to Lumumba's arrest at Sankuru. He voiced the feelings of the other European settlers and the Belgian soldiers, with fingers itching on the trigger that, 'the Prime Minister be transferred to Katanga where he should be judged as a common criminal.' But this was five weeks later.

Reporters were unanimous that when they saw Lumumba at Leopoldville he had already been 'roughed up'. He had lost his glasses, his shirt was stained and there was a clot of blood on his cheek. The Associated Press gives the following account of when Lumumba was brought before the head of the military clique: 'Colonel Mobutu with folded arms watched the soldiers slap and abuse the prisoner and pull his hair.' Further accounts describe the revolting and sadistic behaviour of some of the soldiers: 'One of the soldiers read aloud Lumumba's declaration in which he affirmed that he was the head of state. The soldier rolled the paper into a ball and rammed it down Lumumba's throat ... he did not protest but grimaced with pain when the soldier pulled violently the cord which held his hands tied behind his back ... the journalists were not able to see what happened but they heard screams.'[61]

Despite tight security, it was common knowledge that Lumumba was starved and even denied much needed medical treatment. Such was the growing volume of protest that Mobutu called a Press Conference on 6 December. He answered the criticism by stating that, 'Lumumba at Thyssville has three boys at his disposal. He sleeps in a comfortable bed. The ANC spends 1,000 francs a day for him and his companions. Two doctors came to see him (their reports however were not made known). The camp soldiers did not want to let them in because they were incensed that so much was being done for Lumumba.'[62] But Mobutu refused to allow any one, even UN personnel, to corroborate even one item of the story. It was after the mutiny in the middle of January that a decision was taken to liquidate Lumumba. With the death sentence being passed, Lumumba, Mpolo and Okito, were sent to Katanga on 17 January 1961 for execution.

There are several versions of how Lumumba and his two companions met their fate. G. Heinz and Donnay in their book *Lumumba: The Last Fifty Days*[59] have rendered the revolutionary movement in Africa meritorious service by attempting meticulous investigations in this affair. Although on the available information they offer no conclusions, yet they give various versions. We give three of these.

Kwame Nkrumah in a statement to Reuters Agency on 19 February 1961 said: 'Lumumba and his two lieutenants received orders to leave their Katanga prison on 18 January and were told to pray. While they were kneeling, a Belgian police officer ordered an African to fire on them. The two lieutenants were executed, but the soldier lowered his rifle when he came to Lumumba and refused to fire. The Belgian then reached for the rifle and killed Lumumba.'

The Commission of Inquiry of the UN stated that the prisoners were killed on 17 January 1961, after their arrival in a villa near Elizabethville, and very probably under the eyes of certain members of the government, notably Tshombe, Munongo, and Kibwe. Clues point to Belgian mercenaries, Colonel Hughe, Captain Gat, and Ruys also being present. The UN, however, exonerated completely Union Minière, although there was very strong evidence of its refrigeration plants being used to store the bodies for a time.

The Algerian publication the *Revolution Africaine* writing five years later said: 'Even though there are several versions of the assassination of Lumumba, the same names come up each time, Tshombe, Munongo, Kibwe, the Belgian mercenaries Gat, Michel, Leva and Hughe. Lumumba and his companions were taken to a small isolated house. A grave had already been dug. According to the statements of Lucas Samalenge, Tshombe, Kibwe, Munongo, Kitenge, Sapwe and Samalenge arrived that night at Lumumba's place of martyrdom. Some Belgian mercenaries were there with some Katangese state police who were to be the grave diggers. Tshombe then demanded that Lumumba ask for forgiveness for all his bad actions against Katanga, and also that he recognize in writing the independence of Katanga; and Lumumba flatly refused. He was then savagely beaten up by Kibwe and Munongo. The latter pierced his chest with a bayonet. The mercenaries fired, and Gat finished him off. Maurice Mpolo and Joseph Okito were killed without ceremony.'

A storm of protest broke out throughout the world when these brutal and foul murders were made public almost three weeks later. Africa had lost one of its noblest sons, and Nkrumah, a younger brother. In a broadcast to the Ghanaian people, on 14 February 1961, Nkrumah rightly accused UN officials as well as the imperialist powers of being accomplices of this crime:

Somewhere in Katanga in the Congo – where and when

we do not know – three of our brother freedom fighters have been done to death.

There have been killed Patrice Lumumba, the Prime Minister of the Republic of the Congo, Maurice Mpolo, the Minister in his Government who was elected from Katanga Province, and Joseph Okito, the Vice-President of the Congolese Senate.

About their end many things are uncertain, but one fact is crystal clear. They have been killed because the United Nations, whom Patrice Lumumba himself as Prime Minister had invited to the Congo to preserve law and order, not only failed to maintain that law and order, but also denied to the lawful Government of the Congo all other means of self-protection.

History records many occasions when rulers of states have been assassinated. The murder of Patrice Lumumba and of his two colleagues, however, is unique in that it is the first time in history that the legal ruler of a country has been done to death with the open connivance of a world organization in whom that ruler put his trust.

These are the facts. Patrice Lumumba was appointed Prime Minister by the departing Belgian authorities because he was the leader of the Parliamentary party with the largest representation and was the only Member of Parliament who could obtain a majority in both the Senate and the Chamber. Kasavubu was subsequently elected the ceremonial Head of State, but it was clearly agreed and understood that he should have no more authority or power than has the King of the Belgians in Belgium. This fact, clearly written into the Constitution of the Congo, has been deliberately ignored and distorted by those who have sought for their own ends to give some appearance of legality to the military usurpers and the agents of colonial rule who have illegally seized power in some parts of the Congo.

Shortly after independence the Congolese army mutinied. Patrice Lumumba and his colleagues had to secure outside support from somewhere if they were to preserve the legal structure of the State.

In the interests of world peace and in order to prevent the cold war being brought into Africa, Patrice Lumumba invited the United Nations to preserve law and order. The United Nations insisted that they should have the sole mandate to do this and that the legal Government of the Congo should not obtain that military assistance which would have otherwise been forthcoming from many other friendly African States.

However, instead of preserving law and order the United Nations declared itself neutral between law and disorder and refused to lend any assistance whatsoever to the legal Government in suppressing the mutineers who had set themselves up in power in Katanga and South Kasai.

When, in order to move its troops against the rebels, the Government of the Congo obtained some civilian aircraft and civilian motor vehicles from the Soviet Union, the colonialist Powers at the United Nations raised a howl of rage while, at the same time, maintaining a discreet silence over the build-up of Belgian arms and actual Belgian military forces in the service of the rebels.

With a total disregard of the Constitution, which expressly provided that the President could not dismiss the Prime Minister unless there had been a vote of 'no confidence' in the Parliament, Kasavubu illegally tried to remove Patrice Lumumba from office and to substitute another Government. When Lumumba wished to broadcast to the people, explaining what had happened, the United Nations in the so-called interest of law and order prevented him by force from speaking.

They did not, however, use the same force to prevent the mutineers of the Congolese Army from seizing power in Leopoldville and installing a completely illegal Government.

Despite the fact that one of the most important reasons for United Nations action was supposedly to see that all Belgian forces were removed, the United Nations sat by while the so-called Katanga Government, which is entirely Belgian-controlled, imported aircraft and arms from

Belgium and from other countries, such as South Africa, which have a vested interest in the suppression of African freedom. The United Nations connived at the setting up, in fact, of an independent Katanga State, though this is contrary to the Security Council's own resolutions.

Finally, the United Nations, which could exert its authority to prevent Patrice Lumumba from broadcasting, was, so it pleaded, quite unable to prevent his arrest by mutineers or his transfer, through the use of airfields under United Nations control, into the hands of the Belgian-dominated Government of Katanga.

The United Nations is, on behalf of all its members, in control of the finances of the Congo. It is now two months ago since I personally wrote to Mr Hammarskjold to ask him where the money came from which is being used to pay the soldiers in Mobutu's illegal army. I am still awaiting an answer. One thing is certain, however, this money does not come from the revenue of the Congo. It is supplied from outside by those who wish to restore colonialism in practice by maintaining in office a puppet régime entirely financially dependent upon them.

The time has come to speak plainly. The danger in the Congo is not so much the possibility of a civil war between Africans but rather a colonialist war in which the colonial and imperialist powers hide behind African puppet régimes.

At this very moment Northern Katanga is being laid waste by military units under command of a regular officer of the Belgian army, Colonel Crèvecoeur, armed with the most modern weapons, supplied by Belgium.

Recruiting offices have been opened in South Africa, in France and elsewhere, and wages of over £400 a month are being offered to former German fascist officers and to former collaborators of Hitler and Mussolini in other countries in order to persuade them to enlist in an unholy war against the African people. Where, I ask again, does the money come from to pay these big salaries and to buy all of this modern and expensive armament which is now being deployed against unarmed peasants and villagers?

The rulers of the United States, of the United Kingdom, of France and of the other Powers who are militarily allied with Belgium, must answer these questions.

Why did they express so loudly their indignation when the Soviet Union placed at the disposal of the legal Government of the Congo civilian aircraft and civilian vehicles? Why are they so silent when their ally, Belgium, openly supplied military aircraft and armoured vehicles to the rebels? Why is it that no single Member of the North Atlantic Treaty Organization has on any occasion addressed to Belgium any public rebuke for the flagrant breaches of the Security Council Resolution in which Belgium is every day indulging? Alas, the architects of this murder are many.

In Ghana, we realize the great financial stakes which some Great Powers have in the Union Minière and other industrial and commercial undertakings in the Congo.

I would, however, ask these Powers these questions: Do they really believe that ultimately they can safeguard their investments and their interests in the Congo by conniving at a brutal and savage colonialist war?

Do they realize that they are sacrificing African lives to continue in Africa the cold war at the very time when all powers, both great and small, should be concentrating on the abolition of colonialism and the establishment of world peace?

Patrice Lumumba, Maurice Mpolo and Joseph Okito have died because they put their faith in the United Nations and because they refused to allow themselves to be used as stooges or puppets for external interests.

There is still time for those who have supported this cruel colonialist war in the Congo to change their policy, but time is running out. The cynical planning of the murder of Patrice Lumumba and his colleagues is a final lesson for us all. We cannot ignore the fact that this crime shows every evidence of the most careful preparation and timing. First there came the handing over of Patrice Lumumba and others to the Belgian-controlled authorities in Katanga.

Next there came the contemptuous refusal of these same authorities to allow the United Nations' Conciliation Committee any access to the prisoners. From this came the final proof that the United Nations would not effectively intervene to save the life of the Prime Minister or his colleagues. This was followed by the formation of the so-called new Kasavubu Government and the warning by Belgium to Belgian nationals to leave those parts of the Congo controlled by the legal Government.

Finally came the story so reminiscent of Fascist technique – the false account of an attempt to escape and the death of the prisoners following upon it.

What are the next steps in this plan? The information before me now is that the Kasavubu-Mobutu group has planned an offensive against Orientale Province in an attempt to secure a quick military victory before the Security Council can deal with the matter. My information is that this plan has been made with their full support. Let me issue a most serious warning. Any such action, unless immediately denounced by the other members of the Security Council, will have a profound effect on African relations with the Great Powers.

Our dear brothers Patrice Lumumba, Maurice Mpolo and Joseph Okito are dead, and I ask you all to join with me in mourning the loss which the whole African continent has sustained through their cruel murder. But their spirit is not dead, nor are the things for which they stood: African freedom, the unity and independence of Africa and the final complete destruction of colonialism and imperialism. The colonialists and imperialists have killed them, but what they cannot do is to kill the ideals which we still preach, and for which they sacrificed their lives. In the Africa of the future their names will live for ever more.'[63]

And the Indonesian poet, Anantaguna expressed the same feeling, that in the chants and choruses of those fighting for freedom the memory of Lumumba will never die. Written on the day that Lumumba died he wrote:

The news came early in the morning.
    Lumumba is dead
    Lumumba is dead
Anger split the whole world asunder.
    A worker shouts:
    who can murder my age —
    the rails of the trains
        the length of the light of the sun
    we are all Lumumba
Lumumba.

    A peasant stamps his feet
    the people never die —
        the heart is in the paddy
        growing along in struggle and song

Freedom that's Lumumba
Lumumba,

The news came early in the morning
    Lumumba is dead
    Lumumba is dead
    the earth shook
    the revolution marches on.

    Long live Lumumba.

At his death, Lumumba was 36 years old.

22

CONCLUSION

THE class struggle which has broken out with such storms in Africa in this decade of the seventies erupted with great force in the Congo. It brought out in rapid succession the polarization of class forces so that the oppressed and exploited could see who were their real friends, and who their enemies. It is thus that the Congo experience becomes important. Everyone engaged in the African Revolution must assimilate the experiences here, for it is the Congo in essence which is still being fought out all over Africa.

Lumumba said in his farewell letter to his wife: 'They have corrupted some of our compatriots and bribed others.' How true and prophetic. Lumumba was one of the first African leaders to see and point out the new phenomenon – that the leaders of national movements in whom the people had reposed so much trust and confidence, could be bribed, corrupted and put their honour up for sale. All that one could add to this penetrating observation is that, those corrupted belonged to, or had aspirations to belong to, a particular class, namely the bourgeoisie.

Marx and Engels profiting from the historic experience of the Paris Commune in 1871 said that 'the working class simply cannot lay hold of the ready-made state machinery and wield it for its own purposes.' Lenin rightly interpreted this to mean that it was no longer a question of a transference of bureaucratic machinery from one hand to another, but that the working class had to 'smash' it. The breaking up of the bourgeois, state machinery is an essential part of every people's revolution. This applies particularly to those African countries which are striving to use their political power to secure economic independence. In doing so, they come face to face with the machinery of the state.

It has been widely believed and accepted that with independence imperialism granted political power, but retained economic control. But this is a contradiction. The political structure must reflect the interests of the dominant economic class. Events in the last decade in Africa have proved that political independence and economic subservience is a dangerous illusion. What the imperialists gave on granting independence was not real political power, but state machinery designed to facilitate the continued exploitation of the masses.

Engels pointed out the relationship between the bourgeoisie and the state machinery when he said that wealth exercises its power indirectly, but all the more surely, first by means of corruption. Imperialism was able to corrupt top layers of the state machinery in Africa from the civil service to the armed forces. Its task was facilitated in that it could bribe its way on the cheap, because the top layers in fact had no property, let alone capital, but whose appetite for accumulation was voracious.

Lumumba in 1961 was a voice crying out in the wilderness. And yet ten years later the experience revealed the staggering dimensions of this very corruption in the West African Republic of Guinea. Perhaps one of the greatest single events for the African Revolution was the unmasking, exposure, trial and confessions, of the top leaders of the Republic of Guinea's Party and government who in 1970 allied themselves with the international bourgeoisie to overthrow the socialist-oriented government of Sékou Touré. Just who these traitors were was revealed by Camille Camara, cadre of the Parti Democratique de Guinée (PDG) when he said that the members of the fifth column were some of the closest associates of Sékou Touré, and held top positions in the party and government. Secretly, they tried to sabotage the economy, and told the people that the economy was lagging because of the policies of Sékou Touré. These same people, however, were some of the most vocal defenders of socialist policies. It is indicative of the growing maturity of the African Revolution that in Guinea these elements using armed force, were met by the armed force of Revolution, a people's militia, and thus suffered a major defeat. Sékou Touré describing this historic period in the African Revolution said it was 'a struggle of classes'. On the one hand in Guinea stood the workers and peasants with revolutionary intellectuals, and on the other, a section of the bourgeoisie linked with imperialism to overthrow the conquests of the Revolution.

The lesson then from the Congo, as well as in Guinea and elsewhere, is that the struggle against imperialism for economic independence must involve equally a struggle against the bourgeoisie, which is tied to the apron strings of imperialism. Kwame Nkrumah in his *Class Struggle in Africa* says: 'The bureaucratic bourgeoisie, the inheritors of the functions of earlier ruling classes, are closely connected with foreign firms, with the diplomats of imperialist countries, and with the African exploiting classes. Although not a cohesive élite, they are in general dedicated to the capitalist path of development, and are among the most devoted of indigenous agents of neocolonialism. Their education and class position largely isolate them from the masses.'[64]

The African bourgeoisie in the immediate post-independence period was essentially bureaucratic, with a small trading class. In other countries it would rightly be classed as the petty bourgeoisie. But there was no indigenous class above it. Essentially it was at the beginning a bourgeoisie without any property, let alone capital. Having arrived late on the historical scene at a time when the world was already going socialist one can understand its desperate haste to catch up with history. Its thirst for accumulation was insatiable. Its tastes were bourgeois as were its aspirations. But unlike the classical bourgeoisie this bourgeoisie was not involved in production, for the profitable sectors of the economy were already cornered by the foreign super monopoly corporations. Therefore all that they could sell was their political power and influence in the state machinery. This is what they gave to imperialism in return for money and goods. The state machinery thus became one large cesspool of corruption. It became the fashion to put oneself up for sale in order to get rich quickly. Cabinet ministers could be bought for a 20 per cent fee.

In Guinea, the victory of the forces of revolution against counter-revolutionary attacks on 22 November 1970, unearthed the extent of imperialist ramifications inside Guinea as well as the methods employed by imperialism. One is struck at the patience of imperialism. Diagne Costa, one of the traitors, confessed that the strategy of the fifth column was:

1. to denigrate systematically the government of Guinea in every place;
2. to discourage the cadres in the party and state;
3. to sabotage the economy all over the country;

4. to undermine the confidence of the national currency;
5. to demoralize the masses so that they lose confidence of the government;
6. finally to overthrow the government.

President Sékou Touré divided the fifth column into six categories. The most important one consisted of 'ministers, regional governors, ambassadors, army officers, civil servants, top party officials.' These traitors revealed in their confessions, which make sordid reading, that they were involved directly or indirectly in the plots to overthrow the government. Fourteen Cabinet ministers were involved. These men linked themselves with the French and West German Secret services while publicly they identified themselves with the socialist policies of Guinea. They sat and deliberated in the highest organs of the state and party on behalf of the people, and took decisions only to reveal them the very same night to the enemies of their people. The confessions reveal that the groundwork for a coup is laid years in advance by imperialism. The military junta that takes over in a coup is just the tip of the iceberg. The bribes were high by any standards. Ministers got an outright grant of 200,000 dollars and then were put on a monthly payroll of 5,000 dollars a month.

The military men were asked to use racialism and put tribe against tribe in the army on questions of salary and promotions. They were to organize thefts of ammunition, incite soldiers to mutiny, and increase antagonism between the army and militia. On the civilian front, West Germany was to be given favoured treatment in contracts and they were to oppose the influence of Russians and Chinese.

The experience of the Congo and Guinea has shown that One has divided into Two. The national movement that once united all the classes is split. A tiny section of the National Front, the bourgeoisie, has allied itself to its former imperialist masters. Just as the bourgeoisie in the Congo, Guinea and throughout the contested zones of Africa, sought out their allies beyond the national boundaries, so too have the workers and peasants. In Senegal and Ivory Coast, in defiance of their governments whose sympathies were with the fifth column, workers and students braved the bullets and batons of the police in order to extend hands of solidarity with their class brothers in Guinea.

In this most intense class struggle in Guinea, concretely expressed in the life and death fight between revolutionary and counter-revolutionary forces, hitherto sentimental and sacred ties were destroyed. Brother betrayed brother, and they fought each other. Moslem slaughtered Moslem and Christian fought Christian. Close and personal friends found themselves in opposite camps, ready to kill. The Guinean fifth columnists tore aside the bonds of religion, family, brotherhood, and allied themselves with total strangers with different language, religion and culture. Money destroyed those bonds, and their class interests turned them against their own people.

This is the lesson for the whole of Africa to learn before it is too late. When the line of division is called, respective classes will seek out their allies.

How was it that the Guinean people were able to foil the plots of the combined forces of West Germany, France, Portugal and the Guinean bourgeoisie? The answer lies in the high degree of political and military mobilization of the people, and the acute political consciousness of the cadres of the PDG. Without fear for their own positions they denounced their own leaders who were in league with imperialiasm. Then, when the real testing time came in the hour of invasion they acted on their own to defend their sacred soil and their revolution, sometimes in defiance of their own leaders. The high degree of political consciousness can be gauged in that Guinea has 8,000 party cells which meet every week to discuss anything from international to local issues. The party exercised control of every section of national life. Thus the soldiers regarded themselves first and foremost as party men in uniform. In contrast to others, their loyalty was first and foremost to the party, and then to their superior officers.

In the Congo this same class struggle ended in temporary

defeat for the revolution. The victory in Guinea ten years later, shows the maturity of the forces of Revolution in Africa. In the Congo, as in Guinea the state machinery in the course of the struggle has been shown to be not only a coercive and oppressive organ but also the institution which imperialism and its lackeys, the African bourgeoisie, use to suppress the Revolution.

There is no prospect of any serious headway being made by any people for the elimination of exploitation of man by man unless the state machinery is given a thorough shaking up from top to bottom. Elements of the bourgeoisie must not be allowed to take over power in the name of the people and use this very power through the state machinery to suppress them. In Africa, Asia and Latin America, the national movements cannot stop halfway. The very process of movement against political domination of the colonial powers sets in motion other forces so that it has to move out of the narrow orbit of bourgeois nationalism, and become part of the socialist revolution. It is just this that imperialism feared would happen in the Congo, and that is why it mobilized all its strength to prevent it from happening. The stakes were indeed high, for it was not only the riches but also strategic raw materials like uranium and cobalt that figured in the planning. It is not that far-sighted imperialists wished to murder Lumumba, but that his indomitable will and his unyielding spirit gave them no alternative. Lumumba alive could well have taken the Congo along the socialist road.

No leader had against him such a formidable list of opponents and enemies. Not only were there the Tshombes, Mobutus CIA agents within the UN or as 'experts', but also his castigators at the UN. He had further to contend with UN troops who came under the guise of liberators and became in fact an army of occupiers. Some African countries in whom he had reposed trust turned out to be his enemies. Yet such was Lumumba's confidence in his cause and in the power of the people that he gave battle and knew that he would win in the end.

Few leaders have been able to travel the entire gamut of political relationships as did Lumumba. Within just one year, such was the speed of events that a whole era had been traversed. He accepted the parliamentary challenge believing that the rulers would honour the verdict of the people, and then saw how the rulers cynically cast it aside when they found that parliament could not be used for their own interests. He was beginning to understand the role of the military and the necessity for having peoples' armed forces. He saw through the various manoeuvres of imperialism, and that the independence of many of the African States was just a sham. Finally, he understood through trial and error, and through the most bitter experience, that objective conditions in the Congo were such that the only true path to liberation was by way of armed struggle. From a political leader he had accepted the fact that he had to become a revolutionary fighter.

It has been one of the standard practices of oppressors to project a false image of those whom they have hounded, persecuted and destroyed. It has been the same with Lumumba. Not only has he been falsely represented, but his very assassins and persecutors now claim to be his true successors. But in doing so they have taken great care to present Lumumba as a mere reformer, a well-meaning person who strayed from the right path and not a fighter and revolutionary. It is a bloodless, colourless and emasculated Lumumba who is being projected to the rising generation. They defaced him while he was alive; they try to do so now when he is dead.

Lumumba was a fighter by temperament and occupies an honourable place in the gallery of great revolutionaries. Like many others, his death has made him alive as never before in the hearts and minds of millions of oppressed and exploited throughout the world. The new unspoilt and forward-looking generation of African youth looking for ideals, and heroes of the best that humanity can offer, have readily adopted him and made him their own. Lumumba lives on, more than many a living leader.

APPENDIX ONE

Letter Sent to the Secretary-General of the United Nations

by President Kwame Nkrumah on 7 December, 1960
on the Congo Situation

Your Excellency,

I have the honour to inform you that I am greatly disturbed by continued worsening of the situation in the Congo and the extent to which everything seems to be getting out of hand. From its inception, I have always considered the situation in the Congo not only as a vital issue to international peace but also as a challenge to the United Nations demanding the cooperation and support of all its members. In full realization of this, Ghana decided to act in concert with the United Nations and placed her armed forces at her disposal in the hope that it was only through that Organization that the threatened anarchy and chaos could be prevented.

Your Excellency may recall that since the beginning of the incidents in the Congo, I have always placed my advice at your disposal. On my instruction, my Chief of Defence Staff made an on-the-spot study of the situation and in a personal report to you on July 21, stated that, 'The immediate and also the long term possibility of getting the country back to normal hinges on the re-training and the re-disciplining of the Force Publique. One of our first tasks must be to bring the Force Publique under proper control. Everything must be done to persuade the Cabinet to cooperate in the action taken to re-train and re-form this Army, but whether or not the cooperation can be obtained, United Nations must do its duty.' Subsequent events have proved how right the Chief of Defence Staff was in his assessment.

In my reply of 19 August, to your message of 18 August, I reiterated an important point in my General's observations as follows:

> In regard to the more general issue you will note the General's view which I fully support that if the Ghanaian troops in Leopoldville had the type of full support from the United Nations which he suggests, the Ghanaian Army are certain they could bring the Force Publique in Leopoldville, under effective control in one week.

Today, this Force Publique whose potential for exacerbating the situation was so clearly realized at the outset is being used by interested powers which finance and maintain it, to prevent the due process of parliamentary democracy and to arrest the Head and other Members of the legitimate Central Government.

Dr Bunche in his reply to a memorandum by my Chief of Defence Staff on 21 August 1960, stated: 'I agree, of course, that the re-organized and re-disciplined Congolese National Army, is the most, perhaps the most, vital problem.' Yet little or nothing has been done to solve this problem.

In your telegram to me dated 27 August, Your Excellency referred to the 'extremely dangerous factor constituted by the undisciplined and leaderless soldiers remaining over from what was once the Force Publique. These troops if stirred up and turned against the United Nations will obviously make any constructive action by the Organization impossible.' Today, the Force Publique has not only been stirred up but it is advised, organized and financed by Belgian and other financial, imperialist and colonialist interests to oppose the United Nations and the last vestiges of legality in the new Republic.

I am firmly of the opinion that the course of events in the Congo would have been different if the diagnosis I outlined to Your Excellency in my communication of 6 September had been followed. In this message, I stated that 'This situation has been caused by the fact that the United Nations are not in a position to enforce law and order which we always thought to mean existing law and constitution.' I went on to state further that:

> The essential thing now is for the Security Council to reconsider the position so that the territorial integrity of the Congo can be preserved without intervention of any countries other than those contributing to the United Nations Forces.
>
> Ghana is in favour of a solution on the basis of the first resolution of the Security Council and which will exclude intervention from outside.

Had a solution on this basis been pursued we would not be in the present position of forgetting almost completely that the United Nations went into the Congo to help the Central Government, at its own request, to maintain law and order and uphold the territorial integrity of the country in the face of foreign intervention. The warning was not heeded and today world public opinion has been confused by the agents of imperialism into accepting the thesis that the tragedy of the Congo is essentially a domestic dispute between rival leaders.

With sinister methodical efficiency, these agents proceeded to discredit certain members of the United Nations who have contributed forces to the Congo Operations. Official and unofficial propaganda was aimed at the removal of Ghanaian and other forces and creating an anti-United Nations feeling so that at the moment any United Nations Official is liable to be arrested, searched and subjected to other indignities. When it was decided to remove the Ghanaian forces from Leopoldville, I stated in my message to you through my Permanent Representative on 17 October, that 'Quite apart from the political objections to the move at the present time there will undoubtedly be serious security repercussions in Leopoldville.'

This warning was reiterated in my telegram No. GN.622 dated 27 October. In this telegram I referred to various grave incidents which had occurred in Leopoldville including the arrest of 176 supporters of Lumumba and the disarming and detention of soldiers known to support Lumumba. I stated that the civilian population including foreign traders were frightened because of the constant rumour that they would be attacked as soon as Ghanaian troops left Leopoldville. In the light of these incidents I informed you that I could not share your confidence that the disorders in Leopoldville were not in any way related to the projected move of Ghana troops.

You disagreed with me on important points in your telegram of 31 October, but on 20 November, I was forced by events to inform you that:

Reports reaching me clearly indicate that the situation in Leopoldville is deteriorating since Ghana troops left Leopoldville. As you yourself may be aware hundreds of Belgians are returning to the Congo daily and are indulging in intrigues of all kinds calculated to hamper United Nations operations in the Congo and to enable them to restore their influence and control in the Congo. There is sufficient evidence of reprehensible Belgian activities to discredit the United Nations troops, and create disaffection amongst sections of the Congolese people against units serving under United Nations command in the Congo.

Since the removal of the Ghanaian troops from Leopoldville there have been, as I foresaw ample evidence of acts of violence and lawlessness.

I have frequently advocated a strong and effective military command for the United Nations Forces in the Congo. The ineffectiveness of this command has been clearly demonstrated by the trend of events, and by the fact that, in spite of the original intention to restore law and order in the Congo, the United Nations has slowly but surely lost the initiative in its task, and we see the United Nations Secretariat tamely acquiescing in this position. In Leopoldville, at least, the Organization is now being dictated to and pushed around by Mobutu's band which is actively maintained by the Belgians and other foreign agents, although it is itself incapable of controlling its own troops. I therefore urge most strongly that the military leadership of United Nations Forces be changed immediately and is taken over by commanders who have sufficient experience and judgement to re-establish dignity and confidence in the higher direction of the United Nations military affairs.

It can, of course, be argued that acts similar to those being committed at present by Mobutu's men, were earlier committed by the old Force Publique.

As you are well aware I have frequently urged that the influence of the so-called Congolese Army should be eliminated from politics and I did my best to persuade Lumumba to use restraint in this direction.

I would not object, nor I feel sure would my African colleagues, to a firm statement that United Nations Command will ensure that the ANC is eliminated from the political argument. But to effect this now will require much greater firmness than has hitherto been shown by the United Nations military command in the Congo. Nor can I imagine that Premier Lumumba would not dispute the right of the United Nations to re-establish proper law and order. This could not be construed as interference with the internal affairs of the Congo: it has now been amply demonstrated that internal affairs cannot function at all under existing conditions.

I am also distressed by the fact that United Kingdom Royal Air Force aircraft flying in support of the Ghana contingent at present in Kasai, have not been allowed to land at Leopoldville. Surely the whole authority and purpose of United Nations efforts to restore peace in the Congo cannot be allowed to suffer from the irresponsible acts of individuals. These aircraft are used solely for the support of the Ghana troops, which have done so much to restore peace in Kasai, and there can be no possible excuse for obstructing their work. It is absurd that in circumstances such as this the

United Nations Command in the Congo should find itself incapable of eliminating unwarranted interference with aircraft carrying out their normal duties under the auspices of the United Nations.

The intrigue and activities of the colonialists and imperialists against the independence of a young African State are carried on with such effrontery and cynicism that those who want to see cannot be deceived. Mr Dayal's report came in time to give adequate warning to the dangers facing our sister young African State in the return of Belgians obsessed with revenge, spite and utter contempt for African aspirations. Unfortunately, powerful States came to the defence of their imperialist friends and statements were issued challenging the accuracy and objectivity of Mr Dayal's report. Needless to add that these very detractors were at one time so keen on saving the United Nations that they considered the slightest criticism of United Nations action in the Congo as treason.

Now we see the legal Prime Minister of the Congo in chains with the sovereign Parliament of his country surrounded by arms and men undoubtedly maintained by foreign interests.

Do you, Your Excellency, not see bitter irony in the fact that the Government and Parliament which invited the United Nations to assist with the restoration of law and order have been forced to the wall by the systematic use of violence before the very eyes of the United Nations High Command?

How can we the small nations within the United Nations maintain confidence in this Organization when we witness situations which remind us of so vividly today of the fate of the League of Nations? It seems quite clear that your own position as Secretary-General is seriously compromised and undermined by the apparent inability of your military representatives in the Congo to carry out faithfully and effectively the Resolutions of the Security Council.

I have made these points in a genuine effort to call a serious warning against a situation which might lead to grave consequences for the future peace of the world. Timely action is theerfore necessary. I, on my part, must confess that I am utterly dismayed at the prospect of the United Nations finding itself in opposition to the attitude and policies of the Government which invited this Organization to the Congo to give it much needed assistance for the restoration of law and order. Can anyone genuinely say that a so-called administration which attempts to function by means of violence and disregard for all the principles of international relations be considered legal authority for the day-to-day running of the affairs of a new independent state?

Now, Your Excellency, I would like to ask a few simple questions. How are the ANC being paid? Who is paying them? Where is the money coming from? Who supplies the Kalondjists with their arms?

The United Nations' claim that it is in the Congo to maintain law and order could at least make some meaning if the claim were established on the side of the legitimate Government, but I am appalled to see that a band of armed men which has prevented the functioning of the elected Parliament of the Congo is being loudly applauded from the roof tops of the Western world as an organization which can be relied upon to bring about peace and security in a confused State. Your Excellency, the United Nations Organization is the last bulwark of peace and the hope of the new Independent Sovereign States of Africa. I am therefore concerned that nothing should happen to disparage its efforts and reputation in the eyes of the world.

In the Congo today the United Nations is facing its first real challenge since its establishment, and I am most anxious that you, as its Chief Agent, should have full opportunity to consolidate and reinforce its power and authority in accordance with the Security Council Resolutions on the Congo. This must be done effectively by the immediate and unconditional release of the legal Prime Minister, Mr Patrice Lumumba, the clearing out of the Belgian *saboteurs* of Congolese independence who have infiltrated back into the Congo, and by eliminating the connivance of the colonialists seeking to perpetuate their control and domination in the Congo. Unless everything is done quickly to re-establish the political *status quo*, namely, the release forthwith of the legitimate Prime Minister with those members of his Government now under arrest, and the restoration of the normal processes of parliamentary democracy, there will be left a tragic mess in the Congo for which the United Nations cannot, I fear, escape responsibility.

I avail myself of this opportunity to renew to Your Excellency the assurances of my highest consideration.

KWAME NKRUMAH
President of the Republic of Ghana

APPENDIX TWO

Broadcast on the Congo Situation

By Kwame Nkrumah, President of the Republic of Ghana on
15 December 1960

THE situation existing in our sister nation, the Congo, has now
become so critical that I consider it my duty to speak to you tonight
to remind you of the facts which led up to this crisis, to warn you
of the dangers that today face not only the Congo, but Africa and,
indeed, the whole world, and to suggest to you the only possible
measures that I believe can be taken to avoid these dangers.

As we all know, independence was formally handed over by the
Belgians on the 1st July this year to the legally constituted government of the Republic of the Congo with Mr Kasavubu as its
President and Mr Patrice Lumumba as its Prime Minister, duly
elected by the Congolese people.

On 13 July, barely twelve days later, mutiny broke out within the Congolese army, acts of violence spread throughout the
country and the machinery of government was brought to a stand-
still. Then Mr Lumumba, on behalf of his government, appealed
to Ghana and to other Independent African States for military
assistance to help restore law and order. An appeal was at the
same time made to the United Nations.

In response to this appeal, a Ghana military contingent was flown
to Leopoldville forthwith, followed shortly afterwards by units of the
Tunisian army. The United Nations Military Command was established some days later, and took over control of military operations.

Within a few weeks of our arrival in the Congo, it became
apparent that the Belgians were infiltrating back into the country
and were re-arming the Congolese troops for an attack upon
the Government, and every effort was being made by them to
paralyse the United Nations Command. I personally warned the
Secretary-General of the United Nations about this and pointed
out to him that the only possibility of getting the country back to
normal hinged on the re-training and re-disciplining of the Force
Publique, a force of some 25,000 men stationed in various parts of
the Congo. After my Chief of Defence Staff had made an on-the-
spot study of the situation, I further requested the Secretary-
General to consider urgent measures for re-organizing the United

Nations Command in the Congo so that it might become more effective in its all-important role, and stated that if the Ghanaian troops in Leopoldville could count on the full support from the United Nations, I was certain that they could bring the Force Publique in Leopoldville under effective control in one week.

Nothing was done. Instead the Force Publique was allowed a free rein to run riot, to be financed and maintained by those with vested interests and by colonialist and imperialist powers, to prevent the due process of parliamentary democracy and, finally, to arrest the Head and other members of the legitimate Central Government and Parliament of the Congo.

Proposals were then made to transfer the Ghanaian troops from Leopoldville to other parts of the Congo. I made it clear that I did not consider this a wise move at all, since Leopoldville is the capital of the country and I considered that if law and order were firmly established there, it would serve as an example for the rest of the Congo.

Regardless of my advice once more, the move was carried out. A few days later, Mobutu and his armed band, morally and physically supported and directed by the Belgians, challenged the authority of the United Nations Forces in Leopoldville, attacked our Embassy in Leopoldville (against all diplomatic practice), waged verbal war against Ghana and other independent African States who had come to the aid of the legitimate government of the Congo, put the legally elected Prime Minister Patrice Lumumba under house arrest, and finally ran him to earth, arrested him like a criminal, publicly humiliated him, locked him up and severely manhandled and maltreated him.

Reiterating Ghana's position in the Congo situation, I have now requested the Secretary-General to consolidate and reinforce the power and authority of the United Nations in accordance with the Security Council Resolutions on the Congo, and suggested to him that to do this effectively, the legal Prime Minister, Patrice Lumumba, must be immediately and unconditionally released from prison, all Belgians who have infiltrated back into the Congo to sabotage the independence of that country must be sacked forthwith and all colonialists who are seeking to control and dominate the Congo must be eliminated. Unless these conditions are fulfilled and the normal processes of parliamentary democracy thereby restored, the tragic mess which will result in the Congo will be the inescapable responsibility of the United Nations Organization. What is happening in the Congo is a test case for the United Nations. If they fail in their mission there, who will feel able to place their faith and confidence in the United Nations in the future?

In short, there must be immediate United Nations intervention in the Congo to forcibly restore law and order.

I have many times declared that the only hope for world peace lies in the United Nations. Throughout this whole Congo crisis, Ghana and all other independent African countries, in spite of their first-hand knowledge of the evils of colonialist and imperialist intrigues and the way to deal most effectively with them, have stood loyally by the United Nations Command. They have had to stand as silent witnesses to imperialist intervention in the internal affairs of the Congo, forced to turn a blind eye because their orders forbade them to do otherwise, watching the ground being carefully removed from under the feet of the Head of the Government who had invited them to the Congo and whom they are supposed to be protecting.

It pains me to say that the United Nations has been a bitter disappointment and has far from justified our hopes. For one reason or another, it has talked, vacillated, hesitated and delayed until its whole presence and action in the Congo have been reduced to a farce – and a very expensive farce, at that. At the moment several States which have contributed to the military personnel of the United Nations Operation in the Congo are so deeply disillusioned by the United Nations' inability to take any constructive action in the Congo, that they have decided to withdraw their forces. Whilst Ghana sympathizes with these nations as far as their disappointment in the United Nations is concerned, I nevertheless appeal to them to reconsider their decision to withdraw their forces from the Congo. Ghana believes sincerely that the withdrawal of the troops will spell immediate doom to the Congo and will precipitate the anarchy which all well-meaning countries are anxious to prevent.

If the United Nations troops are withdrawn from, or forced out of the Congo, there will be an imminent risk of civil war, of the Spanish type, which could last for many years and would put the Congo back a century or more. If civil war broke out, those countries that have vested interest in the country will vie for power by supplying arms and ammunition to the various factions taking part, and this can eventually transform the inapparent Cold War into a terrifying Hot War.

It is obvious that none of the States whose troops are now serving in the Congo is desirous of pursuing any independent action calculated to worsen the present situation in the Congo. That is why some of them have intimated that they are prepared to reconsider their proposal to withdraw their troops, but only on condition that the United Nations Command will cease to be a mere passive onlooker to the acts of rampant lawlessness perpetrated by Mobutu and his gang.

The impotence of the United Nations Command in the Congo is not deliberate. It has been imposed upon it by the exigencies of those with vested interests in the country and by colonialist and imperialist intrigues and sabotage. From the very beginning of the Congo crisis, I have warned against the infiltration of the Cold War into Africa via the Congo or elsewhere. With our declared foreign policy of positive neutralism and non-alignment, I have regarded with increasing suspicion the sincerity of foreign intervention in the Congo. I warned the Secretary-General of the United Nations of my fears in this connection in early September, saying that I believed the situation had been caused by the fact that the United Nations was not in a position to enforce law and order which we had always understood to mean the existing law and constitution. I urged him to ensure that the Security Council should reconsider the position so that the territorial integrity of the Congo could be preserved without the intervention of any countries other than those contributing to the United Nations Force.

Many people would like to make excuses for the United Nations. Others would prefer to mince their words to please the ears of their economic patronizers. Neither of these platitudes are of any help to this great world organization which was created by men of goodwill and foresight to prevent tribulation to mankind. I believe that only genuine and constructive criticism of its action, whether it be in the Congo or elsewhere, can make any valuable contribution to the strength and purpose of the United Nations. Only by this means can it realize its mistakes and profit by them. I do not doubt the fact that the United Nations has had many difficulties to face in the Congo; but I believe most emphatically that these difficulties only became insurmountable because the United Nations has refused to surmount them or has delayed for so long that other things have stepped in to prevent it doing so.

The United Nations has failed to maintain law and order in the Congo because while it has been standing by rigidly adhering to its principle of non-intervention in the internal affairs of the country, the Belgians have, under the very nose of the United Nations Command, acquired stooges and quislings to carry out a flagrant and brazen sabotage of Congolese independence, aided and abetted by those whose chief and only interest in mankind is exploitation and profit, and who hope to share the Congo booty.

But has the United Nations strictly observed this non-intervention attitude throughout? It is clear that it has not. It was the United Nations, in fact, which prevented Patrice Lumumba, the legal Prime Minister of the Congo Republic, from entering and using his own radio station. It was the United Nations which stood by while a rebel, put up as a leader by the Belgians, took it upon himself to put that head of government under house arrest.

Had the United Nations forgotten completely that it went into the Congo to help the Central Government, at the request of the Head of that Government, to maintain law and order and to uphold the territorial integrity of the country in the face of foreign intervention? If the United Nations has become confused about the origin of its mission to the Congo, how much more must public opinion be confused, egged on by the agents of colonialism and imperialism, until it is beginning to believe that the tragedy of the Congo is essentially a domestic dispute between rival leaders.

Too much over-simplification is being brought to bear on the interpretation of Article 2(7) of the Charter of the United Nations which prohibits interference in matters which are essentially within the domestic jurisdiction of member states.

The very presence of the United Nations Command in the Congo suggests some degree of interference to which the lawful Government of the Congo headed by Mr Lumumba consented before inviting the United Nations into the Congo. Having already interfered, therefore, in securing the arbitrary arrest of the legitimate Prime Minister and the neutralization of the Central Government, how can the United Nations now decide to remain inactive? Must one be led to the conclusion then, that the United Nations entered the Congo merely to change the existing government in defiance of every conceivable electoral principle?

The same Article 2(7), under which the United Nations is seeking to justify its inaction, ends by stipulating: 'but this principle shall not prejudice the application of enforcement measures under Chapter VII'. Chapter VII points out that whenever the attention of the Security Council is called to the existence of a 'threat to peace, breach of the peace, or act of aggression', the Security Council can have recourse to measures of compulsion, despite the fact that the matter is within the domestic jurisdiction of any state.

Now, the question arises: who should call the attention of the Security Council to such a threat to peace? In addition to Member States of the Organization, the Secretary-General is empowered to play the role of an informant. Article 99 says: 'The Secretary-General may bring to the attention of the Security Council any matter which in his opinion may threaten the maintenance of international peace and security.'

If the Secretary-General really believes that the continued detention of Mr Patrice Lumumba constitutes a threat to peace, in that it can lead to civil war which, in turn, could bring about a world war, then it is for him to recommend to the Security Council that such necessary measures should be taken to settle the disputes in the Congo. This should be done immediately to salvage United Nations prestige, despite rivalries, subterfuges, colonialist and imperialist intrigues and manoeuvres.

This, in my opinion, is the only method of restoring law and order in the Congo. For to permit the Belgians with their imperialist and colonialist allies to continue to support and rearm Mobutu against Lumumba and his supporters (and be assured that he has many), is to defy constitutional authority, to allow Belgian power to creep back and to invite the disaster of civil war.

It is because of this view point that I am being charged with officious intervention in, and meddling with affairs in the Congo. How can Ghana pursue an isolationist policy in African affairs, when she is committed to a policy of African unity?

Why, in fact, did we go to the Congo? Why have we sent our men to distant lands far away from their families?

We are in the Congo because the freedom and independence of our compatriots are at stake. We remember only too well the price we paid to secure our own freedom and independence. We know, too, that freedom is not worth having if it has to be surrendered to foreign domination and control, whatever form it takes.

You will recall, also, that when Ghana became independent in 1957, I proclaimed that our independence would be meaningless unless it was linked up with the total liberation of Africa. As long as there is a single vestige of colonialism on African soil, we must remember that we ourselves cannot claim to be free. What the colonialists and imperialists succeed in doing to our brothers and sisters in the Congo by using stooges and quislings who are prepared and willing to sell their country for a mess of pottage, they will not hesitate to repeat in Ghana and in other parts of Africa.

That is why we are exerting every means in our power, denying ourselves every comfort if necessary and counting no cost too great, to assist our brothers in the Congo. The stand that we have taken, and will continue to take in the Congo situation can only be understood in the light of our unflinching determination to fight all forms of colonialism in Africa.

Fellow countrymen:

In order to resolve the present unfortunate impasse in the Congo, I recommend with all the sincerity and urgency at my command, that the United Nations should take the following actions, and to do so without a moment's delay:

ONE – To completely disarm the Mobutu gang and all other non-United Nations Forces, and to eliminate them from politics.

TWO – To arrange for the immediate and unconditional release of the legal Prime Minister, Mr Patrice Lumumba, and of all other members of his Government as well as the members of the legally constituted parliament, who are also under arrest.

THREE – To restore the normal functioning of the legitimate Government and the elected parliament of the Republic of the Congo; in other words, the parliament which made Lumumba the Prime Minister, and Kasavubu the President, should be made to reconvene and function normally.

FOUR – To enforce the immediate evacuation of all Belgian military personnel and officials from the Congo.

FIVE – To assume authority, as a temporary measure, for the internal affairs of the Congo, to enable law and order to be restored.

SIX – To arrange that the United Nations Command in the Congo is assigned to an experienced soldier who can take firm action.

SEVEN – To form a United Nations Committee composed of Afro-Asian countries to investigate the sources that are financing and supplying arms and ammunition to Mobutu and his gang.

Countrymen: In the event of the United Nations failure to comply with these proposals in conformity with the provisions of the United Nations Charter, it will be my bounden duty to secure, with the assistance of the other African States, the establishment of an African High Command to take immediate action to restore law and order so that the legal government, headed by Premier Lumumba, can operate. Good night.

REFERENCES

Note

1 *The Communist Manifesto*, Karl Marx and Friedrich Engels, Pelican Books 1967, pp. 83/4.
2 The same, pp. 84/5.
3 The same, p. 84.
4 *Congo, my Country*, Patrice Lumumba, Pall Mall Press, 1963, p. 99.
5 The same, pp. 100/101.
6 *Class Struggle in Africa*, Kwame Nkrumah, Panaf Books, 1970, p. 12.
7 The same, p. 56.
8 *FEDACOL Courier Africaine*, No. 35 July 1959.
9 *The Congo: Staff Problems in Tropical and Sub-Tropical Countries*, Julian Kasongo, Brussels 1961.
10 *New York Times*, 23 January 1960.
11 *Vers Independence du Congo et Ruanda Urundi*, A. A. Bilsen, p. 176.
12 *Congo, my Country*, p. 7.
13 The same, p. 9.
14 The same, p. 3.
15 The same, p. 112.
16 The same, pp. 4/5.
17 The same, pp. 1/2.
18 The same, p. 145.
19 The same, p. 8.
20 The same, pp. 32/3.
21 The same, pp. 43/4.
22 The same, p. 17.
23 The same, pp. 27/8.
24 The same, p. 81.
25 The same.
26 *Congo, my Country*, p. 130.
27 The same, p. 132.
28 The same, pp. 160/61.
29 The same, p. 161.
30 The same, pp. 167/8.
31 The same, p. 121.
32 The same, pp. 120/21.
33 The same, p. 122.
34 The same, p. 116.
35 The same.
36 *Challenge of the Congo*, Kwame Nkrumah, Paperback edition, Panaf Books, 1969, Introduction p. xv.
37 Proces Verbal du Executif de la Conakat: Seance du 20 Janvier 1960, unpublished.

38 *Political Awakening in the Congo,* Rene Marchand, p. 222.
39 *Class Struggle in Africa,* Kwame Nkrumah, pp. 59/60.
40 The same, p. 59.
41 The same.
42 The same.
43 *Le Probleme du Katanga: Courier Africain* 4/3/1960.
44 Engels: Speech at the Graveside of Karl Marx. Marx Selected Works, Vol. II, p. 167.
45 *Lumumba: The Last Fifty Days,* Heinz and Donnay, p. 18.
46 *Conflict in the Congo,* Thomas Kanza, Penguin African Library, 1972.
47 *External Pressures in Africa Today,* Mckay Vernon, p. 63.
48 *Class Struggle in Africa,* Kwame Nkrumah, p. 51.
49 *Challenge of the Congo,* Kwame Nkrumah, p. 42.
50 The same, pp. 41/2.
51 The same, pp. 30/31.
52 The same, p. 46.
53 The same, p. 51.
54 *Congo, my Country,* Foreword, pp. xv/xvi.
55 *Challenge of the Congo,* Kwame Nkrumah, pp. 61/3.
56 The same, p. 62.
57 *The Congo Since Independence,* Catherine Hoskyns, O.U.P., p. 292.
58 The same, p. 306.
59 *Daily Telegraph,* 19 January 1961.
60 *The Congo Since Independence,* p. 269.
61 *Lumumba: The Last Fifty Days,* p. 47.
62 The same, p. 64.
63 *Challenge of the Congo,* Kwame Nkrumah, pp. 129/33.
64 *Class Struggle in Africa,* Kwame Nkrumah, p. 61

Books by

KWAME NKRUMAH

CLASS STRUGGLE IN AFRICA
HANDBOOK OF REVOLUTIONARY WARFARE
AFRICA MUST UNITE
TOWARDS COLONIAL FREEDOM
DARK DAYS IN GHANA
AXIOMS OF KWAME NKRUMAH (Freedom Fighters'
  Edition)
NEO-COLONIALISM: THE LAST STAGE OF
  IMPERIALISM
CHALLENGE OF THE CONGO
CONSCIENCISM
GHANA: Autobiography of Kwame Nkrumah
VOICE FROM CONAKRY
SOME ESSENTIAL FEATURES OF NKRUMAISM by
  Editors of The Spark
I SPEAK OF FREEDOM
REVOLUTIONARY PATH

Pamphlets

THE SPECTRE OF BLACK POWER
THE BIG LIE
GHANA: THE WAY OUT
TWO MYTHS
THE STRUGGLE CONTINUES

Trade terms 35% discount on the U.K. published price
                40% discount for orders of 500 copies or more

Panaf Books Limited
243 Regent Street, London WIR 8PN